No Dead Air

No Dead Air:

Career Reflections from the TV Executive
Who Saved Barney the Dinosaur from Extinction

LARRY RIFKIN

© 2021 by Larry Rifkin

All rights reserved. This book or any portion thereof may not be reproduced or used in any manner whatsoever without the express written permission of the publisher except for the use of brief quotations in a book review.

ISBN: 9798526377355

My deepest gratitude to all my colleagues and associates, named and unnamed, for sharing with me your extraordinary talents and making our time together so rewarding.

And, of course, to Carmelita, Leora, and Wade for a home filled with laughter and love to return to each night.

My gratitude extends to Carmelita, Harriet Unger and Attorney Malcolm Stevenson for their careful reading of this manuscript.

Special thanks to Gwenn Fischer and Sarah Lange Davis.

Prologue: My Dad

It was early on a cold New England Sunday morning in the mid-1960s. A boy walked gently into his parents' room, where they both were sound asleep. He tapped his dad's shoulder and told him the one thing that no radio station manager would want to hear. "Dad, you've got dead air." His dad responded, "Wake me in ten minutes if we're still off the air."

Back in those days, this meant that the religious ramblings of the most vociferous preachers and ministers were rolling off a reel-to-reel tape spool at one of the many AM stations, trying to honor their commitment to provide community programming.

The station 1240 WWCO was one of several in Waterbury, Connecticut, a city of over one hundred thousand people. It was a great center of industry for most of its modern history. Known as the Brass Capital of the World, with companies such as Anaconda American Brass, Chase Brass and Copper and Scovill Manufacturing, Waterbury could proudly boast that, in many ways, it was able to skirt the Depression based on the ingenuity of its people and its coveted products.

When immigrants stepped off the New York docks seeking work, many were told to go to Waterbury. There was good work there for someone who had the will to learn and a strong back.

In fact, Ken Burns featured Waterbury as one of the four cities in his World War II series on PBS. He shared with the world that at one time Waterbury was indispensable to the nation because no American soldier could go to war without bringing something from the city. In 2006 much had changed regarding the city's fortunes when he did this tribute to the ingenuity of Waterbury and three other cities as his way of finding a fresh angle into the most reported on and visualized war in history.

If you were new to the city or had been in a slumber for the many years in between, you might ask what went wrong. In some ways it is a common story but with characteristics unique to Waterbury.

The city had been beleaguered since the 1970s when, like many cities, deindustrialization took a mighty toll. And that toll was most apparent on the people and their spirit, and ultimately the facades and the bones of buildings and neighborhoods that once represented Waterbury's indomitable spirit.

Waterbury went from a working-class mecca, where a factory job could virtually ensure a stable middle-class life rich in fellowship, fraternal, and religious associations, and diverse in ways that cities were because those with needed skills emanated from many cultures to a city battered and beaten and in ways forgotten and, worse, ridiculed and further diminished because of the betrayal of its political leaders.

The *Republican-American*, a local newspaper, won a Pulitzer in the 1920s for exposing the political corruption of the Frank Hayes administration. Waterbury could rise above the corruption at that time because of the strong backbone it had from its estimable business community. However, no longer buttressed by business leaders who could shelter the city from such political storms, it was powerless in the face of the petty political criminals feeding off the carcass of the once proud city.

While my mother, Edith, was born and raised in Waterbury, my dad,

Wallace, came to the city from Brooklyn, New York. They were a wonderful couple. My father was the baby of his family and my mom the "virtual" baby. My mother had a beloved sister, Frances (Fagie, as we called her), who was the true baby of the family. She had Down syndrome, and as was the standard practice at the time, when my grandparents died, she was institutionalized at Southbury Training School, then considered a model facility in nearby Southbury, Connecticut. While beloved by her brothers and sisters, the logic at the time was that a residential setting, warehousing, was best for all. Fagie reminded us that each life has potential. She was a proud Girl Scout and a loving aunt. Her life and soul were a window into the human spirit of a very impressionable boy like me.

Wally (King) Rifkin as a young man

It was my sense that my parents' sisters and brothers admired this young couple because their love was genuine and deep, and their contentment in this place was real. As true as that was, for my dad it led to a general distancing from his family in New York, except for wonderful visits to my grandmother, Dora, at her apartment in Brooklyn and, in season, her cottages at the beach in Far Rockaway. He was woven into the tight tapestry of my mom's family as everyone lived within blocks of one another and got together every week.

While some people grow up to become someone, I inherited so much of my dad's persona that an apt title for this remembrance might be *To the Radio Station Born*. I was a "radio brat." That simply meant that the boss's kid, at a very tender age, imagined he knew who should and should not be on air. The kid had a loud mouth even then and, more importantly, the ear of the boss.

"Make this your last day" was my father's motto. Lacking context, you might think he was the stereotype of the overbearing boss. In truth, he was just the opposite. He was beloved by all—employees, the community as emcee of important community events, and even competitors.

Well, perhaps I exaggerate, which is early in the book for that, because form would suggest that I reserve that to buff up my career. This reflection is about recounting a life that might hold some purpose for you, the reader, as you count strikes and balls in your turn at bat.

There was one man who I am sure was none too happy with my dad. It was the poor soul who got the call that fateful Sunday morning when the radio brat woke his dad, at his request, a second time. "You're still off the air."

So my dad made the call to the control room using the "Hot Line", and what he heard on the other end was more dead silence. You see, a telephone does not ring in a radio studio lest you interrupt every live broadcast. It only lights up. That is hard to see when your eyes are closed and you are sound asleep. And on this Sunday morning, the announcer was. Suffice to say on that day, for this infraction, my dad did "make it his last day."

It was always a mystery to me how my dad wound up in Waterbury. In New York, he was a child actor and did stints on radio, at the legendary WOR Radio 710, with "Baby" Rose-Marie and Jackie Cooper. And legend had it that he was the choice to play the part that Leo Gorcey strong-armed the producer to assign to his cousin, Bernard Gorcey, in the classic New York–based series *The Bowery Boys*.

He had a gorgeous, velvety voice, reminiscent of Mel Tormé or William B. Williams, a radio idol of the era. He would lend his voice in song on his "Fun at Four" show, which he used to launch his initial Waterbury career on WATR 1320-a station that would come to define an anchor for both of us in our lives centered around Waterbury.

My career took on many of the dimensions of my father's, and after establishing a larger media palette on which to create, I yearned to return to my roots—his roots—and was able to do that as I mirrored some of the same joy he felt being in the center of a small universe where what you did and said affected people you could see and talk to every day.

But the road back to that place was a long and interesting one. It found me unexpectedly in the middle of one of the greatest media phenomena of the late twentieth century, all without ever leaving home.

Despite the notion that to have an impact on a national scale in broadcasting required uprooting yourself and moving to either New York or Los Angeles, I somehow found a way to do it by way of a different playbook. And I found myself in an orbit well beyond my dreams or intentions, working on projects that would reshape various aspects of the television industry and put me in contact with celebrities and dealmakers I never felt I would be able to run with. But what kept me grounded was the fact that I could recall my dad and his contentment at being the big fish in a little pond, going to work every day in the center of it all.

While my mother's commitment to her large Waterbury family might have kept my father's career from taking on a trajectory much higher than what—to the world—he achieved, it gave me the rich roots in which to nourish my desires and find a place that will always be home.

As I walked down the venerable Bank Street in Waterbury and took the elevator at 65 Bank Street to the two floors occupied by WWCO, the excitement and joy being "the" rock station in the market was intoxicating.

I recently came upon ratings for WWCO, back in the day sourced by "Metro Waterbury Pulse." The report read, "In Metro Waterbury, if you're looking at men and women 18–34 you'd better look at WWCO," and continued," More men 18–34 listen to WWCO than all other Waterbury radio stations combined." The station had 62 percent of men and 58 percent of women in that desired demographic. It was a monster.

My dad recognized that a radio frequency, as limited as the allotment was in that era, performed many vital functions in a community. You were called upon to provide news, weather, and a sense of place and be a promoter of good causes and a trendsetter as you shared what was happening in the popular culture.

Looking back on his role as general manager of a local radio station, it was not that he would not have wanted me to aim higher than that. It is my sense that the satisfaction he got from his work made it such a desirable destination as a career. It did not feel like work at all. It just seemed like so much fun. He could feel the impact in the community and hear his vision being played on car radios everywhere. This need to be heard is what drives all of us in this industry. Whether it originates out of fear or out of ego, I don't know.

I can tell you that having spent literally thousands of hours before an open mic, and a good portion of that on camera, I always imagined that my best performance was my last one. I feared that I could not rise to that level the next time. What would you call that? Angst, self-doubt, lack of confidence? Perhaps it represented the way I motivated myself.

I wanted to meet the high standards my dad set for himself and his staff. He was the man who left me this legacy of professionalism and dual capacity to both perform and lead other creatives. He never transmitted it overtly or pushed me in this direction. That was not his way, nor was it necessary. He just lived his life, and I thought it was much more interesting and cooler than what the other dads did.

In the cluster of houses adjacent to where I grew up, when our family was intact, I could look out at the homes of the superintendent of schools, police chief, editorial page editor of the local newspaper, and other luminaries, but no one's career could top my dad's job for excitement and cultural relevance.

We might only have been renters, living in a duplex at 135 Leffingwell, with my dad making $12,500 a year, but I envied no one for their higher station in life. Dad ran the station everyone I knew listened to.

In his capacity as an entertainer and radio personality, he emceed many of the historic moments Waterbury experienced in the 1950s and 1960s. Two stand out.

One was the fateful evening of the "Flood of 1955" in August of that year when the great star Rosalind Russell came back to her hometown to introduce her new film, *The Girl Rush*, to her adoring fans. The event took place at the historic State Theater, long since demolished. It was a magical night that included Russell's costar Gloria DeHaven. Given the limits of meteorology in those days, the force about to be unleashed on the unsuspecting citizens of the region would be profound.

Legend has it that my dad who originally came to Waterbury to be the program director of WATR 1320, took a rowboat about a mile down road, not river, to the station's location at the time on Meadow Street in downtown Waterbury. He remained on the air for three days to deliver vital, life-saving information to the station's audience.

My dad also was the emcee of one of Robert Kennedy's events during a visit to Waterbury to carry out a promise that his slain brother, John F. Kennedy, had made to the people of Waterbury because of the city's amazing support for him. Nearly thirty thousand people were in downtown Waterbury to catch a glimpse of the charismatic Bay State senator at three in the morning on the Sunday before the 1960 presidential election. He returned to Waterbury as president in 1962 and promised a cheering crowd of fifty thousand people that he would return to Waterbury during "the last week of the 1964 campaign." And while an assassin's bullet made that pledge impossible to honor, there is a plaque that reads, "His pledge was fulfilled," on the site where he spoke in 1962. Bobby Kennedy came to Waterbury in 1964 to dedicate that plaque, and my dad emceed the event.

Dad's stage name, Wally King, will never be known to the rest of the world, but it lives in me. And perhaps that is why well into my career, an encounter with greatness in my field was less than satisfying.

On September 10, 2007, I found myself on the stage of the city's other historic theater, the Palace, now restored, emceeing the preview of the

Waterbury-focused episode of Ken Burns's WWII series, *The War*. And joining me on stage for the event was Ken Burns himself.

It was a wonderful evening to be sure. As a point of privilege, with deep pride and great care, knowing the audience and our shared angle on seminal events in Waterbury's modern past, I took literally less than ninety seconds to reflect on my dad and his place in the city's public life, with particular emphasis on the Flood of 1955. But it was relayed to me that Mr. Burns was getting a bit anxious, wanting his customary (and much deserved) place on stage at the center of attention.

I had learned over the years how to engage an audience on their terms, where they are from and what they care about. It was another lesson well learned from my dad. Damned if I was going to let it go by. If not me, in that moment, then who or when?

With all due respect to Ken Burns, the greatest documentarian of our day, I could not leave the stage that night without affirming my dad and his life.

Grandmother Dora Rifkin, parents Wally and Edith, and Grandmother Esther Kravitz on Larry's parents' wedding day

Chapter 1: Done Too Soon

How great it was to be a preteen in the early 1960s and feel as if you were old enough to understand what an amazing time you were living through but not old enough to have to take a stand or risk being swept under by the tide of history. I had a great view of it all.

Living in Connecticut, so close to New York, I was within striking distance of the vanguard of emerging forces. Here I was in a city, diverse and fractured enough to be part of these social changes, just miles up the road from the Black Panther trials in New Haven. Yet it felt far enough removed to allow me to spin my cocoon of watchful observation rather than full immersion.

Under the tutelage of my father, I was able to sense the turbulence of the time. I was given a view of the culture through the music he played and the personalities he nurtured on his radio station, all the while feeling he would provide safe passage wherever the social convulsions of the time would lead us. Little did I realize how much he, in that moment, was preparing me to engage in a life of curiosity about social and cultural forces if I just stayed open to it all.

As general manager of the rock station in the city, he had contact with all kinds of folks who were working to promote this new culture. At the very time my friends had to contest their parents' old attitudes and musical tastes, let alone access to the family's record player, my father was turning me on to Crosby, Stills & Nash, and we were experiencing the change together. As a New Yorker, he was open to people with different points of view and backgrounds.

I wanted to be a drummer. In one sense my dad had doubts about my musical inclinations. I imagine most parents would prefer melody over rhythm for their musically inclined child if only because one is pleasing and the other, for a long stretch of time, is just noise.

Reluctantly he let me take lessons at Mobilio Music Store while he wondered aloud to Bob Mobilio, a fine musician and store owner, whether the "$3 a lesson" was worth it. I can categorically say yes although not because I was able to attain great skill on the kit. Capable and intermediate might be the most apt description of my drum skills.

So many elements of my life took shape in that small shop. I can still recall its glorious clutter and the excitement of young guys like me who wanted to quicken the pace of our lessons so we could start our own bands. We all imagined what might await us in terms of fame and fortune—and girls, of course.

With a few friends in grammar school, we started that garage rock band like every other Beatles-inspired kid at the time. Who can forget playing at one of the YMCA's weekly dances for a dollar a man or getting our heads handed to us in a battle of the bands against, of all groups, "The Caskets"?

Our band was called The Avengers, named after Diana Rigg, the female protagonist in the classy British series of the day and subject of all our desires.

The legacy of the Mobilio Music Store was that perhaps the best teacher I ever had, Ed Montana, taught there. His primary vocation was selling cigarettes. Employing a great sense of humor, he dangled his favorite brand of smokes behind both ears. Ed convinced you that if you worked at it, your potential was unlimited. A ploy to squeeze weekly threes from the old man, you ask. Perhaps. But to this day, when I open my old "Syncopation" book and see his notes, I pause, reflect, and smile. I keep his picture behind an old Gretsch drum kit on my music stand.

My tie to the Mobilio Music experience and Ed was further enhanced when I had my first Slingerland kit refurbished by Art Benson years later. His Dynamic Percussion shop in Manchester, Connecticut, became a stand-in for Mobilio Music as an adult.

To get to Dynamic Percussion to visit with Art, I had to make a forty-five-minute trip from home. Purchasing a piece of equipment was merely a cover story for hanging around and sensing that moment when I was first introduced to music, thanks to Ed, Bob, and my dad.

It was at Mobilio Music where I realized that music was the most pleasurable emotional form of expression available to me. My career and my life from that point on would be interlaced with music. Whether it was wasting endless hours listening to it, playing it on the radio, producing it for television, helping introduce a whole new generation of children to it, or finding myself starting a garage rock band, again at the age of fifty (picking up where I left off in eighth grade), music was, and continues to be, my constant companion.

Garage rock band 2.0 represented another fanciful part of my life's story. I found myself on a stage playing to a crowd of one hundred thousand people and twice having internationally known bands "open" for us. Like Forrest Gump, I have had an uncanny ability to place myself in situations I never imagined possible. There is an explanation that goes beyond earned musicianship, which will be revealed later in these pages.

I had the great fortune of producing television programs with some of the great performers of my era such as Carole King, Bobby Vinton, Ronnie Spector, and Gene Pitney. And twice I traveled out of the country to produce international music specials.

Early on, the expectations I had for my musical adventures revolved around playing the hits on AM radio or having long conversations with record label salesmen, such as the legendary Merv Amols of Capitol Records, who became a friend of my dad. He regaled him with stories about the performers and the records. I wanted to hear those stories.

There are young people in this era who are criticized for their inability to launch or leave home. I guess I was ahead of my time.

While my elder sister, Marcy, had a great sense of wanderlust, which found her taking excursions to Europe or living in a communal setting and making homes in states across the country, I was content with—one might say committed to—staying around. And so rather than attending college in Boston at Emerson College, where I had been accepted, or even in Storrs, Connecticut, the main campus of the University of Connecticut, I decided to attend a branch campus on Hillside Avenue in Waterbury. How parochial was that? Did I not want to be away from home, or did I have a sense that I still had more to learn from a man whose path I was sure to follow? As it turned out, time was of the essence.

I have never been a terribly adventuresome spirit. I understand the confines of my comfort zone, and while I am willing to explore those limits to their fullest, I am not one to embrace the murkiness of the unknown.

My shield in this lifetime has been a personality that projects much more confidence and worldliness than really exists. Anything I have been able to do has required a stable place and set of relationships, my parents and wife chiefly, to allow me to achieve a measure of success.

While others experimented with alcohol and drugs, I found a way to limit their place in my life to a point where they have been negligible. As I look back, I can imagine that this propensity has limited my social and business opportunities. Never one to sit at a bar and throw back a few, I set about to outwork those with far more ability and more desire to associate on a social level. My personal command and control center was equipped with an uncanny ability to get people to project whatever they wanted about me.

While this next bit of information may seem irrelevant, I offer it as illustration. In both grammar school and high school, I won the same superlatives—best personality and class chatterbox. Incongruous, you say. I talked a lot, and when people liked it, I would respond. And a lifetime of talking, both on and off the air, about topics with which I was familiar and more than a few that I improvised has given me something to write about.

Larry at Grandmother Rifkin's bungalow in Far Rockaway, New York

So in the warm cocoon of the city I loved and the comfort of home, I began my university life in a setting just steps beyond my high school and barely different in any manner. However, in 1971, by the end of my freshman year, something dramatic had changed. On April 17 of that year, my dad died of a congenital heart condition, which would have been repairable given a few more years as the odds improved markedly for the heart surgery he needed. His cardiologist considered it too risky to attempt at the time.

While I was out on a date that Saturday night, no mention of such a great loss for our community was allowed on the air lest the "radio brat" hear it and be devastated by the news.

I picked up his satchel and moved on, with no plan, no design, just his example of a life well lived. Now what would I do with it? My mom, a widow at forty-six, and I carried on. It was so much harder for her. I had the benefit of the selfishness of youth, the search for young love, and the potential of a career ahead of me. She had experienced so many touch points with her beloved husband. What awaited her?

I know I was company for her, but was I really able to internalize her grief? Or was I too consumed with the fact that my father and I would not work together in radio? That he and I could not own a station or two as "and son"? Or was I so focused on the pressure of his idealized legacy in my mind and in our city that it forced me to abandon near-term broadcasting goals and find my own space? Was I up for the challenge? I had my doubts. Throughout my life, like music, doubt has been a constant companion.

Chapter 2: You're Fired

Why do we go to college? Is it to widen our aperture on life or to acquire skills directly applicable to a particular job? As I went through the experience, my dilemma was that while a law degree would have made the most sense, arguing and entertaining in the court of public opinion really was much more interesting to me. While toying with the idea of law school, I chose to use college as a place to stay on a less-than-precise course in the communications field.

It was clear that while I was imbued with my father's instincts for broadcasting, I had doubts that I ever could attain what he had. He had an incredible voice that had all the undefinable qualities of the most polished performers of his day. He had gained near-universal respect for his talents and genuine humanity. So it was up to me to determine if I was up to the challenge of staying within that lane and failing miserably or finding my own approach.

Like so many of my decisions in life, I found a way to make my own path.

The owners of WWCO, the station my dad managed until his death, encouraged me to get my third-class radio operator's license. That piece of paper was required for those recording meter readings on the station's transmitter and its output.

While I had talked a good game about knowing who had the attributes to be on the air, the far more revealing question was "Did *I*?" I was the at-home critic, subjecting all those disc jockeys over the years to my wrath if they fell short in any of the categories this radio brat used on the scorecard: voice quality, entertainment quotients, timing, pace of the presentation, and just whether, to my ear, they had it. And while my father heard me out about the performers he hired, in truth, he had a great ear for talent.

WABC in New York set the standard with its lineup of sluggers from the sunshine-drenched morning man Harry Harrison to the afternoon drive-time king Dan Ingram, and nights in the city that never sleeps were owned by Cousin Brucie, but my dad assembled his own talented crew of strong personalities from sunrise to sundown.

Tom Coffey was a strong morning man with great pipes and the right name for the shift, Jay Crawford and Ray Simone were the housewives' friend (that was the term in the day) in the late morning and early afternoon, and Bob Ruge, "the tiny tot of the kilowatt" as he described himself, was a perfect afternoon drive-time host. The best nighttime host, Mike Holland, was a very gifted disc jockey who later left to make his mark in Canadian radio on powerhouses, such as CHUM in Toronto, Canada. I remember my dad marking the days when Mike would return from his tour in Vietnam to take his place back on the air. As I recall, his reentry was not easy as the images of the gruesome conflict he had endured haunted him for some time.

While often programming executives were not skilled on-air performers themselves, my dad had the advantage of playing that role in the past. I got elevated into an on-air role at WWCO because of my father's legacy, not because of my burning ambition, creativity, and abandon to get on the air.

I find my friend Joe Cipriano's story much more compelling. He wanted to be on radio so badly that he sneaked into my dad's station in his early teens, hid from him when my father dropped by in off-hours, and was befriended by various DJs, who let him hang around the studio. They showed him the ropes and encouraged his desire to get on air as a precocious teen. With that temerity, he put everyone on notice that he would not be denied. He has since gone on to be one of the most requested voice-over talents in America through his sheer determination and talent to succeed. He's a nice guy in a business that often leaves such rare specimens as roadkill. As the voice at various times of the Fox network, *CBS Evening News*, and Food Network, he is in the midst of a great career with much to reflect on as he does in his book, *Living On Air*. I encourage you to read his story firsthand to understand the path he took to make such a mark in this industry.

We grew up in the radio business at a time when you were required to strip away any of the characteristics that might make you less appealing to an audience. Key among them was your ethnicity. From a radio station perspective, anything that might turn away a listener was not good for business. Does he sound too (fill in the blank)? Can a woman deliver an audience, or would that turn off the guys? Does he have a quirky speech pattern?

The first choice many of us had to make was determining what our stage name would be. Fortunately my dad did that for me. While I would assume his adopted surname, King, I affixed Brian, my middle name, to it. I never have been a big fan of my own first name, perhaps because its fame was derived from the least interesting of The Three Stooges. Brian King was born—though that name would be short-lived. And Larry King, the soon-to-be radio and TV icon, could have his own identity in South Florida until he gained the attention of the whole nation.

In Joe Cipriano's case, he took on the name Tom Collins when, as a confident teen, he assumed the estimable position of afternoon drive-time DJ at WWCO. He was clearly the rising star. Later he would go on to have an identity crisis of sorts so that he could work in an adjacent market. Continuing his ascent in the industry, he became Dave Donovan while working simultaneously in the Hartford market at WDRC. Audience identity with one station was sacrosanct at that time.

Recently there has been more cross-pollination so that Charlie Rose, for instance, could, before the fall, have his PBS and CBS identities simultaneously. Or Anderson Cooper can work for both CNN and CBS.

Joe's slight of name penchant made it a difficult choice for a programmer in Washington, DC, who was trying to make a hire with two finalists in mind, only to find out that they were one and the same person. I told you he had moxie. When Joe had the desire and resources years later, he gathered the quirky group of disc jockeys he had left behind in his pursuit of voice-over gold in Los Angeles for a reunion in Waterbury. It was commemorated with photos and comments on a Facebook page dedicated to "Remembering Super Music CO" years later.

At the reunion, while I could remember a lot of faces, weathered with time and the imbibing that goes along with many bounce-along moves to obscure markets, it was harder to remember all the names because each of us had two or more. Joe never engendered the envy and jealousy you might have imagined due to his success because of his respect for those who spin records three hours a day, whatever the size of the audience. We each sensed he had earned all the accolades from when he was fourteen to this day.

With what is now a relic of a bygone era, my third-class permit in hand—one of the few certifications of professional standing in my career—I set out to dip my timid toe in the water. In 1973 and 1974, I continued going to college and working in radio at WWCO part time on weekends and as a fill-in. To me, it was the best of both worlds. I was a college student, and I felt the sky's the limit because I was doing professional, not college, radio. If one went badly, well, I had a fail-safe.

As to whether I could mirror my father's career, I could postpone or defer that reckoning because I posited that I was doing something else. And while my dad went to NYU for two years, a rarity at that time, my commitment was to go on in school to create as many options as possible for my future without committing, and perhaps failing, early on.

Before I graduated from college, I got fired for the first and, as it turned out, only time in my career from this part-time announcing position. My sound was just not right for the new program director, Joe McCoy. To quote Bob Dylan, "One day the axe just fell." It was a gentle rebuke. Joe was a man who knew what he wanted in terms of sound, but my style just wasn't it. If I recall, it went something like this: "Man, you're just not right for the music. I think you'd be better doing news." Later Joe McCoy became the longtime programmer at WCBS-FM, the oldies station in New York, so who am I to question his judgment? Looking back, he probably was right.

At the time I remember feeling devastated. It confirmed my doubts about my future.

Chapter 3: WATR Always

I decided to go on for a master's degree in my quest to maintain all options. Little did I know that it would be critical to my career. I never really knew why I should pursue it at the time. Maybe I sensed that had I stopped with a bachelor's degree, the options available to me would have been limited. And that speaks to following your instincts. As much as self-doubt has dogged me about my abilities for most of my days, the counterbalance has been an innate sense that my instincts about people, life situations, and ability to put matters into context are true.

Presently there is a whole industry out there that helps you figure out how you're wired and how you can know your innate self. To me, it was just something I had in me that I took for granted. A trust in it never betrayed me. While I was not impulsive in my decision-making, I was resolute. After parsing different options, if it felt right, then I would go with it. Key in my decision-making over the years has been how an action might look from an ethical standpoint and how it might appear under intense scrutiny.

In broadcasting we are challenged on many occasions to make tough choices about the ethical nature of what we say or do since it all goes so public. Perhaps the adage "You eat with that mouth" should be emblazoned on a station door. In many cases broadcasters must straddle various thin lines of what is right and wrong.

Controversy challenges us to make sense of the opposing views without necessarily tipping the scales. We are compelled to acquire listeners and viewers with provocative subject matter without making the act of looking through the peephole the point of the exercise. We have our sympathies about groups long abandoned by our society but do not want to lose our ability to bring objectivity to reporting on even the dispossessed, if required. And most often we are challenged by the influences of money and sponsorship as we determine whether to look at or away from a topic.

Simply because the excitement surrounding the industry is so great, it attracts storytellers, literally and figuratively. You can imagine how clear a compass you need to avoid true north disappearing on you.

I cannot imply that obtaining a master's degree in corporate and political communication at Fairfield University, a Jesuit-run institution, was instrumental in gaining that ethical foundation, but given that some of the professors were men of the cloth, it didn't hurt. It seemed like a perfect degree for someone who wanted, perhaps, to do politics, public policy, public relations, or broadcasting. Admittedly it was cobbled together. It was emblematic of my career in hindsight.

I admired my uncles, members of the "Greatest Generation," who made money by being industrious and unafraid in their pursuit of sustaining their families. They had no pedigree from a university to make an introduction. It was word of mouth that they had the desire to work and enough life experience to reapply it to pursuits as distant from one another as selling cars and then on to making neon signs. They reinvented themselves constantly and out of necessity.

I never credited myself with the gifts of reinvention, but I have played many variations on a theme and taken full advantage of the connections among them. If the broad theme were communication, then all the experiences I have had, seemingly disparate, make sense and have woven a tapestry of an interesting career.

I am writing this memoir not because what I have done is singularly important or groundbreaking but because it is singularly me. And lacking a prodigy's gift or an immense natural talent, say in mathematics or athletics, the rest of us must, like a deft running back, find those seams in the obstacles that life presents daily and run to daylight. Otherwise, we will be consumed by fear and feelings of inadequacy that play out in so many harmful ways for the individual and society.

I will forever wonder whether my father's passing early in my life pushed me to a better place in creating the best version of myself. He left me a guidepost, a great map, a wonderful career option, but still I had to make it my own. And that sense of being given a gift that, when opened, leads to eight other boxes, wherein finally rests the true blessing, is analogous to broadcasting itself.

It is a great gift to have the authority to share your story and ideas with others, but absent making good and ethical decisions along the way, what is the point? If it is fame, celebrity, shock value, "look at me," for its own sake, it is devoid of moral content—a nothing sandwich.

There is nothing wrong with a career spinning records and making people happy. That would have been a good life choice (if I had not gotten fired), but the options I gave myself led to so many pathways I never imagined.

As I pursued the advanced degree, I found a path back from my failure.

I went back to work at the "other" station, not the rock one that my dad managed during the halcyon days of the tumultuous 1960s but the one recognized as the "heritage station" in our city—WATR 1320, where my father's Waterbury story began and mine has never ended.

While WWCO was the emotional anchor to my youth, WATR 1320 has been the epicenter of the community for almost ninety years. It is the station that mature folks listen to, and it has earned and owned the news and information mantle for generations.

My dad initially came to Connecticut to take a job at WATR. He was the program director and host there in the 1950s, and after a detour to Florida for a few years to manage two stations in DeLand, he returned to manage WWCO. So, from the beginning, WATR was a part of our lives, first as my dad's work home and then as a formidable rival with WWCO in the high-stakes competition in central Connecticut.

WATR was built by Harold Thomas. Thomas's daughter married Press Gilmore, who owned and ran the station's properties for many years. Their sons, Mark and Steve, still own the station to this day. Over the years they had several radio properties and a TV station as broadcast assets. Two of WATR's related properties would give birth to two aspects of my career yet unseen. And the anchor, WATR 1320, would later afford me the opportunity to reconnect with my early love of radio and the community that the station serves.

WWYZ, their FM affiliate at 92.5, gave me an inkling into what joy being part of a true phenomenon could mean. And the other WATR, TV channel 20, gave me the opportunity to produce a television event, a first in our state, and the beginning of a relationship with radio's big brother, television.

As it turned out, both opportunities were crucial to me.

Chapter 4: The Peddler

In deciding not to pursue law school, and with an undetermined career in communications awaiting me, I had some decisions to make. Given the imprecise nature of my college track as a political science major and a history minor, I had a gut feeling (and a few gut courses under my belt), signifying that I must reinforce this foundation with some additional credentials.

When I went to the University of Connecticut's main campus for my last two years, I was in a dorm next door to determined types who were preparing for their life's work in pharmacy, medicine, accounting, and other practical fields. While we were at the same institution, we clearly would come away from it with different pedigrees. Their path was laid out before them. All they had to do was follow it and meet the benchmarks, and they could don their smocks and pencil protectors, amass some continuing education credits, and the road ahead had no switchbacks.

In my case, the journey was anything but clear. What do I do next?

My basic goal was to achieve at the highest level possible and gain as many options as I could. I graduated from the University of Connecticut *magna cum laude* and earned a Phi Beta Kappa key, thinking it would unlock another door of some undetermined sort.

Upon graduation, I was sure that I needed more education or at least more paper credentialing greater potential to a prospective employer. It turned out to be one of the smartest moves I have ever made. Almost like a great pool shot, the carom on this move, which I'll describe later in the book, led to a wonderful career—but all by happenstance. I graduated college in difficult times in the mid-1970s. And while I wanted to continue to get my master's degree, I also knew I needed to get a job to help pay for it. My mom, now a widow for a few years, was in no position to keep providing for me.

In the early summer of 1974, before I entered the master's program, I took a third shift position with a friend at a thread factory in Watertown, Connecticut. The noise from this innocuous pursuit was deafening.

I recall not sleeping the night before arriving for our first eleven o'clock shift and seeing a couple driving into the parking lot. It turned out they were husband and wife. One was driving, and the other sat in the back seat. It just struck me that this might not be the only oddity awaiting me. When I heard the call for a lunch break at two o'clock over the loudspeaker, I knew my instincts were right. My friend and I used the time to catch a few winks. As dawn approached and we left this situation, I asked him if we were going to go back for night two. He said to call him when I woke up.

Later that morning, just about a year before the firing I described earlier, I was awakened by a call from Bill Raymond, the WWCO operations manager at the time, asking if I could do the seven o'clock to midnight shift at the station for the summer. It was a perfect segue for me and eliminated the hard decision about going back to the thread factory. Little did I know that this summer shift was the last time I would do a daily radio program until thirty-six years later.

With the possibility of some vague future in politics still looming in my head, I rehearsed the line "I know your pain. I worked the third shift in a factory." It was true, right? The radio shift didn't pay much, but it was great fun and showed my mom that I was trying to do my part.

My mother would do anything for her son, particularly because I was the child who stayed around and kept her company after Dad's death. She did a remarkable job of moving on, carrying the pain of such a profound loss at such an early age. She assumed many different roles and finally became assistant to the head chef at the Cheshire Correctional Institute, a state-run prison in Connecticut. She was loved by all and stepped off this earth as untouched by human pettiness and cruelty as any person I have ever known. Making her acquaintance, her beautiful hazel eyes told you a special soul resided within.

She was beloved by fellow staff and the inmates alike. Upon her death in 1997, an unexpected guest visited me on the day of her funeral. One of the former inmates dropped by to tell me how much his daily interactions with my mom meant to him in the cold, unrelenting din of the prison.

While she had a wonderful family of three other sisters, besides Fagie, and two brothers, none was more beloved by everyone she met. Her elder sister Bertha, a very capable and determined woman, happened to work in Waterbury City Hall in the mid-1970s, and she was privy to the inner workings of the Comprehensive Employment and Training Act unveiled by the federal government to stimulate the economy. It was a period of tremendous economic dislocation, and the term "stagflation" became part of our lexicon accompanied by punishing interest rates and long lines for gas.

My aunt told my mom about the public relations and fundraising associate position at the Easter Seals Rehabilitation Center to kick-start the agency's efforts to heighten its visibility. It was a great agency providing valuable services to those with disabilities in the region. I applied, with her nudge, and got the job.

There are three lessons in this experience. First, never be afraid to acknowledge that you got some help along the way. There is no shame in that. If I did not perform, that initial thrust would not have sustained me in the position as the funding was temporary. The agency would ultimately have to pick up the price tag in the second year. Today we call that networking. Each of us knows someone who can help move our credentials ahead of someone else's or open the door a crack. Sometimes lack of success has less to do with talent and more to do with access.

Second, start your formal work career in an environment where you truly feel the work is important, even if it is not a straight line to where you imagine yourself headed in the future.

Third, create your own vision for a position out of whole cloth. No one had ever done the job before. The possibilities were limitless for one with imagination and drive.

It was there that I recognized I liked hard work. While that might sound like an odd admission, it was revelatory. Some people want to punch a clock and do not look at nine-to-five as a starting point. I did not mind long hours and the added role of "volunteer" that is assigned to anyone working in a nonprofit organization.

When I proved myself and justified to upper management the value of adding to the department, I told my first hire, Anthony Ciarleglio, that he would soon find "it's not all glory." Public relations and development are difficult. The all-too-frequent special events required incredible amounts of planning and time. Tedious organizing, coordinating of people and logistics, and lugging and pacifying participants who felt they were slighted or not given their due were all prerequisites.

I recall a "superstars" competition where one contestant blew up at me over the unsteadiness of a wheelbarrow he had to use or the dance-a-thon from hell that occurred as a snowstorm swelled outside. With 120 participants, some lacking the required pledge money, pizzas coming in from all sections of the city at midnight, dancers dropping to a scant few by dawn, and an hour later a contestant suffering an epileptic seizure—all under an accumulating snowfall—I had the rationale for calling the whole thing off halfway through its scheduled duration.

I became known by Jay Clark, the popular WATR radio talk show host in this city (whose job I would have later in life), as the second greatest peddler in the area—he, of course, being the first. What was I peddling? You name it—special events of all stripes like roasts of major figures in the community; a tribute to the legendary actress Rosalind Russell, whom I referenced earlier hailed from our city; and ultimately first-of-their-kind telethons that would be a harbinger of things to come.

I would do anything to make the rehab center the most visible non-profit organization in the community. While doing so, I recognized my competitive fire to achieve beyond expectations, which I carried throughout my career. I wanted to contribute in a way that would be remembered rather than being thought of as someone who was just passing through. In many ways I think the fear of falling short in that goal was a defining characteristic of my actions. So while I was completing a master's degree, on a part-time basis, I was throwing myself headlong into this position and unburdening my mom in the process.

At the same time, I had a burning desire to get back into radio. I wanted to give it one more shot.

Chapter 5: People Are F***ing to This

As I have taken to writing songs later in life, the song "I Can't Quit Her" was given life years before by Al Kooper, a founding member of the original Blood, Sweat & Tears. Yet it did capture my feelings about another turn in radio. Just because one program director did not like my sound did not mean the next one would think the same.

This is an important reminder. Too often we sign away authority to others to judge our capabilities when in fact we know in our heart of hearts that we have something to contribute.

By the same token, we have a similar ability to conceal things we wish not to share. Take our regular visits to the doctor. I live with this body every day, and the physician sees me perhaps once a year. And about fifteen minutes into that yearly ritual, he has his hand on the door looking for a polite glide path to the next insurance—I mean, disease—carrier. Aside from the truth telling in the blood, I can choose to reveal or conceal an awful lot.

In this case I did not want to surrender my dream to follow gently and lightly in my father's path. I had a no-risk strategy. I was working full time in public relations and fundraising and pursuing an advanced degree. If this were my last act in radio, I had other pursuits that I could tell myself were more important.

I caught a break that would give me my first glimpse into what it is like to be part of a true phenomenon. I define that as something so universally viewed as a success that it confers a certain aura on you, whatever your role in its arrival at the pinnacle.

The mid-1970s represented the dawn of FM radio. Before that, even as the technology had come into use, AM radio was where all the action was. Old habits die hard. Even with FM's superior sound and greater technical efficiencies, radio profit centers were built on their AM presence.

The FM band was used as a holding mechanism for some change to come long into the future. It was being programmed in the early 1970s to classical music aficionados or country music lovers almost as a placeholder until station ownership had the confidence in this new technology to gain an audience. Much of the programming was automated. Such was the case with WWYZ 92.5 FM, a fifty-thousand-watt FM frequency owned by WATR AM 1320.

I had maintained relationships with people there, both as Wally's kid and as an aggressive promoter of the Easter Seals brand.

I heard that they were going to try something different with the FM band and had brought in a program director, Bob Craig, who had been working in Hartford as the midday DJ at WDRC, one of the most celebrated stations in the Northeast. They were serious about this fledgling operation. Bob developed and put on the air in June 1976 what became known as the Natural 92, which was an album-oriented mellow rock station. The blend was original, to say the least. Alongside popular artists such as James Taylor, Carly Simon, and Simon & Garfunkel were juxtaposed deep mellow cuts such as the Pousette-Dart Band, Michael Franks, and Aztec Two-Step.

The secret was that Bob was fastidious in his song selection and maintained an dominating presence as program director; he wanted to control every aspect of the station's unique sound. Every set of music, usually four or five songs, was a cascade from bright and bouncy to the most emotive. The mood it established was unmistakable and rarely duplicated.

Bob did subtle things such as allowing a second between cuts, letting it all breathe, and he picked songs that would touch on the "three *L*s"—life, love, and loneliness. And while he had assembled a talented group of announcers, he kept us on a short leash, ensuring that we never strayed from the reality that music and mood dominated the state of play on the station. We were the connective tissue. Talents as disparate as morning man Glenn Colligan, who has worked in Connecticut radio on virtually every station, and Jack Becker, a cool and serious student of the mechanics of radio, were the bookends.

In between was the class of the bunch and its most iconoclastic character, Ted Sellers, whose given name was Theodore R. Mortensen Jr. He was as kinetic a personality as one could imagine off the air. His vitality and drive were on display as the owner of the region's "Renta Yenta," a franchise dedicated to making your wildest party fantasy come true. He was the wild DJ and MC who could enliven any party.

His gravelly voice was a signature on air. I cannot imagine how hard it was for Ted to stay within the confines of Bob's vision, but he did it using his powerful voice and letting it project personality while the words he could utter were spare. Even with the little he was given to work with, his dynamism stood out on that station without disrupting flow. That was a great talent.

Ted was one of those unforgettable personalities who enters your consciousness often in a lifetime, particularly since he was the first of my professional colleagues who died due to a ruthless form of cancer at the tender age of forty-three.

I somehow found my way into Bob's coterie of announcers for this magical journey as a weekend and fill-in host. It was perfect timing and a moment to reclaim my possibilities as an announcer, with a strict playbook to follow. I was a sponge for Bob's kind of innovation. I saw how his command of the content, precision in its execution, and great care in selecting staff and song made this a special experience for the listener. And it showed.

The Natural 92, among the newly emerging FM stations at the time, made a statement, and its imprimatur was quality, consistency, and originality. I was expected to carry that sound and special mark, no less than any of the full-timers. To put an accent on the "natural" in the Natural 92, I was encouraged to use my real name on air.

Bob Craig liked my sound as did my first programmer at WWCO, Ed Flynn. He was a remarkably talented Connecticut radio personality for about fifty years. I admired his sound as much as anyone on radio. He was old-school like my dad and could carry any broadcast mantle put on him. Fortunately, Ed's path crossed with mine at the beginning and end of my radio career in ways that could not be scripted and will be described later. At WWYZ, I learned how true vision on the part of a programmer could completely turn around the fortunes of a station. I would tuck that away for another day.

Bob Craig was a maestro in a gentle, assertive way. If you played songs out of order, even at three o'clock in the morning, as my friend Steve Erwin can attest, you might get a call reminding you that "he" was listening and that his song set order had purpose and meaning no matter the time of day.

WWYZ became "the" station in our state for this moment in time. It was ever present; you heard it blasting in cars, shops, offices, and restaurants. Even if people did not understand why this station was great and different from others, they sensed it.

The most compelling words Bob ever spoke to the jock crew came at a time when some of the talented group became a little too free with the format and began straying too far from the liner notes he had so carefully prepared. He called a staff meeting to emphasize his point that the discipline he imposed on us was for a reason—to maintain the consistency of the sound. He left us with an admonition that was brilliant and clear. He said, "Before you open that mic, just remember one thing: People are fucking to this."

How much clearer could he make it? Who could ever forget? Message sent.

Chapter 6: Partner

Early on it was clear that I had a certain strategy that went something like this: keep all options open and have some fallbacks.

Even though I was having a modicum of success in all three realms—full-time work, school, and part-time radio job—I wanted to claim something that gave my career a stamp. These undertakings were clearly part of the journey, but it wasn't until I was tasked with producing the first Easter Seals Telethon in Connecticut that this happened.

Before I undertook this ambitious project in 1979, the most important ingredient in my life entered the picture in the form of a beautiful, totally capable young woman by the unforgettable name of Carmelita. While I had been engaged to another young woman for a time, it was my boss at Easter Seals, Charlotte Jensen—a dynamic, no boundaries woman in an era when that was not the norm—who made it clear that Carmelita was the woman I should pursue.

Carmelita was a volunteer at the rehabilitation center who lit up the place as she soaked up hours at an allied health facility in pursuit of her degree. She was dynamic, vivacious, and totally independent. Her father

My wife, Carmelita, and our children, Leora and Wade, youngsters at the time, at the CPTV studios in Hartford

felt that she should not go on to college unless she became a teacher or a nurse. She had other designs and worked as a bank teller and attended community college until she decided she wanted to be a physical therapist and then applied to the rigorous physical therapy program at the University of Connecticut.

She had, and still has to this day, a spirit that takes her into all corners of life looking for new challenges. You would swear I was talking about five different women when describing all the pursuits she has taken on and accomplished. She was given that rare gift of fearing nothing and taking that reckless abandon and kicking her bucket list to the ground many times over. I admire that quality in her. While I often think that I have been driven by fear of failure, she has used curiosity, raw intellect, and attention to detail to demonstrate a motor that few people have.

Just when you thought you could define her as a traditional physical therapist, her primary profession, she went on to become certified in many subspecialties within physical therapy, such as osteopathic manual therapy and lymphedema, the latter requiring certification. She also taught at the university level and followed her fascination with the capabilities of the human body to become a master in the energy work involved in Reiki. Oh, did I mention she does this not only with humans but also with animals?

Speaking of animals, she wanted to pursue her lifelong love for horses, so she bought her own horse and taught herself the art of natural horsemanship. Well into her sixties, she performs rough board, a physically taxing relationship for any horse owner when you are doing the daily care and riding when you can.

Her ten-year stint as a volunteer firefighter in our town, rare for women then and now, signals her limitless capacity to take on and master any challenge.

She is a book unto herself. It was her "at any cost" attitude that gave me the clear path to pursue my career with reckless abandon while she took on a multitude of other roles, including owning a physical therapy practice. Her pedigree and that of those she hired gained her a great reputation with area doctors and her patients. And it was successful by all measures of business performance.

I tell you this to say that work-life balance is really a product of the capabilities of each partner. I just happened to marry someone who really did not need me to define her in any way and was equally, perhaps more, successful than me in her pursuits. The difference was that in her profession, she affected people one-on-one and deeply, while my impact was broader and more in public view. Another partner without her gifts would have changed how I was able to perform in my career.

I was blessed in this moment of the late seventies to be surrounded by incredibly capable women at every turn. That helped me develop a great respect for women in professional roles. Perhaps starting out in an allied health facility dominated by women professionals gave me a different perspective on their capabilities. They played major roles in my work from that point on. I never thought that any piece of business was gender based. I credit that to Charlotte and Carmelita and the brimming self-confidence they each brought to their work. It amazes me that four decades later, movements such as Mika Brzezinski's "know your value" are still necessary for women. Their value was apparent to me early on, and their contributions were integral to any work I was involved with.

After a quick courting period, Carmelita and I were married on January 15, 1978. I knew from that point on I had a partner who would give sage advice, roll up her sleeves and get dirty to get any job done, and be able to embrace my life's work as well as her own. These were all gifts of immense value.

The first test was the design and execution of the telethon, which became the überfundraising and career redirecting opportunity of a lifetime. I embraced it fully.

Chapter 7: A Magnanimous Gift

While there were numerous rehabilitation centers under the Easter Seals banner in Connecticut, including larger ones that had relationships with the major television stations in the state, it fell to us in Waterbury to decide to become the first to join the national Easter Seals Telethon network on a small ultrahigh frequency (UHF) station in our city.

A common theme in so much of my life has been what I will call the WATR vortex. Oftentimes I have been pulled back to this company and its many tentacles. We reached out to the television affiliate of WATR, channel 20, which was housed in the same building, to partner with us in carrying the national Easter Seals Telethon, then hosted by Pat Boone. The national component took up forty minutes of every hour, and we complemented that with twenty minutes of programming produced locally.

It was a big leap of faith for both the rehabilitation center and the television station. Could we raise any money on a low-power UHF station? In some people's mind, the *U* stood for "unable to receive." Could we attract eyeballs and attention? Could we bring TV personalities along to make it a compelling watch? And could we stay on the air for a full twenty-hour period? None of these things were certain, yet we were committed to going forward regardless of the risks. None of us knew whether the time, money, and staff resources focused on this effort would pay off.

Easter Seals nationally assessed our market and projected we would make $40,000 on the event. In today's environment that doesn't seem like an awful lot of money. While I hoped we could do better, it was a gamble. We had to find ways to embrace the television aspect of the activity as the hook to engage all kinds of people in a range of pre-events leading up to the telethon. In effect we built our whole fundraising program for the year around the allure of TV. Allotting airtime to those who supported our effort was the hook, and those who earned it would have a moment in the spotlight. No other local nonprofit could offer that at the time.

My competitive juices began to flow.

Would you rather do a dance-a-thon, a roast of a local personality, and a superstars competition with us or another organization, knowing our events led to a television appearance and the others did not? Mind you that television appearance was on a UHF station with one of the weakest signals in the state. Its big shows were local versions of *Romper Room* and some form of East Coast wrestling. Perhaps we should add Sunday morning Mass to that list. And that presumed you had rabbit ears or a UHF antenna poised ever so carefully to be able to get the signal.

Some of you reading this have memories as vague about UHF television as the picture appeared to many straining to bring in a clear signal. Let us just say that it was not great technology. To give you a sense of the vagaries, a Bridgeport, Connecticut–based UHF station once offered viewers cash if they called in and said they were watching. No one called. These stations were finally given parity with very high frequency stations (channels 2–13 on the dial) with the onset of digital television. So today, among the hundreds of options, those old UHF signals are picture-perfect. Of course, that moment happened to drag them into an environment drenched in choice. In the days described here, people had fewer than ten channels to choose from in most markets.

With radio as my first love, I wonder why the Federal Communications Commission (FCC) did not fully commit to a similar conversion of the AM and FM radio bands into one sound-friendly dial.

To ensure that we gave it our best shot, I was sent to a telethon preparatory meeting in Florida. There we were told how to maximize the impact of a telethon to create "the event" for our community. It was the one time I revisited my short-lived Florida past. We had lived there from 1957 to 1962 so that my father could get his first taste of running a radio station as the general manager.

He came to DeLand, Florida, home of Stetson University in Volusia County, to run WOOO. That's right, "wooo" radio. Its promotional symbol was a Messerschmitt, a cabin scooter or three-wheeled bubble car, built in the factory of a German aircraft manufacturer in the mid-1950s. Afterward he managed the other station in town, WJBS.

After my telethon university sessions, Carmelita, who made the trip with me, indulged me in a visit back to DeLand. I was curious and had to drive by 604 Marion Court, the only home my parents ever owned and one they had to give up, unable to sell it when opportunity knocked for my father back in Waterbury.

Our family left DeLand after five years primarily because my parents wanted my sister to meet a nice Jewish boy in Connecticut. (She ultimately married a fine man, Steve Halsted, who became a Protestant minister.) Their desire for her proved the best thing for me as my potential might never have been realized in the swampy terrain of central Florida.

I came back from that trip ready to make this telethon into a fundraising event our community had never experienced before.

Given our newness and the size of the market, the national Easter Seals made a consultant available to us. In the early stage of your career, you will always find yourself at the knee of a master who imparts wisdom that you are told to absorb like a sponge. And that's likely a truism until you unmask their vulnerabilities and recognize that they are at a consulting stage of life because, frankly, they no longer want to do the hard work required to complete the assignment. I have now lived long enough to have been at the knee of, and then be the knee to, others in this scenario.

In this case I found myself at the knee of a man named John McKillop. He was a debonair, well-coiffed, white-maned Englishman who had the distinction of bringing the Kit Kat candy bar to America. It was never clear to me that the appellation "the Kit Kat Man" was the one he wanted as his enduring symbol of success. I learned early on that you can be recognized or labeled your whole career for one thing that you may find charming or revealing or neither. I loved John, and I think he enjoyed seeing the energy that he had lost somehow reappear in me. I then realized that a consultant throws a lot of ideas against the wall, sometimes never intending for them to land and often forgetting that they originated with him.

When consulting, John typically arrived from New York City on a train in the late morning, and after pleasantries and flirtations with women on staff, he would announce that he'd love a spot of tea or, better yet, to go for an early lunch of fish and chips just down the street at a classic Waterbury hangout, the Big Top. There we would discuss what I had done since we last met, and he would say, "Great idea, Chap." It was then that I would remind him that he first suggested it.

His most memorable contribution was his role as the true adult and sage in the room when we attended the critical meeting to enlist Timex Corporation, headquartered in our region, to become our major sponsor of the event.

My colleagues and I had no experience in sealing the deal. It was John who, while sitting across from then Timex chief executive Bob Weltzien, began using his British flamboyance to suggest that we needed a magnanimous gift as a signal to the giving community, in at least three different iterations, before Mr. Weltzien, who was paid to always have time on his mind, finally called the question in exasperation, "What are we talking about?" and John finally blurted out, "Ten thousand dollars." We walked away with that commitment. Even as a newbie in dealmaking, I came away with a sense that we could have asked for more.

You never really know when the object is of an indeterminate value.

Chapter 8: You Help Crippled Kids

Bucky Dent of the New York Yankees was the Easter Seals ambassador in 1979 after his postseason heroics the previous season—when his home run had helped the Yankees beat the archrival Boston Red Sox for the American League pennant.

He was a handsome guy who used his newly found fame to advance a good cause. He should be applauded for that. I cannot say that he came to the role with a lot of knowledge about what Easter Seals did. That was evident when he came to town to help us promote the telethon and in the car ride from the airport said, "So you help crippled kids." It's understandable that that was the context he had for what we did because Easter Seals used that image to symbolize its services for so many years.

Messaging often requires that you take the most direct route to a donor's heart. We used Bucky's winning smile to produce videos for the telethon showing Easter Seals services at work for the benefit of both the young and old. The facility was abuzz with excitement as a celebrity was in our midst. Little did people realize that the larger celebrity in the room was a member of the production team who one day would be more popular as a celebrity in the entertainment field than Bucky was on the baseball diamond.

A radio friend, Jack Camarda, aka Dr. Chris Evans on the air, started a production company with his friend John O'Hurley. John would later become famous for his role as J. Peterman on *Seinfeld*, as a game show host, and as one of the hosts of the annual Thanksgiving Day *National Dog Show*. In this moment he and Jack were producing vignettes of the various services we provided to be rolled in throughout the telethon. The roles we assume later in our careers can diverge from our initial meandering into various fields. Yet each one is foundational as we build upon it. I am sure John's time behind the camera, focused on the technical aspects of the trade, helped inform his on-screen performances down the road.

This telethon was a first for many of us involved. It was clearly my first time organizing a live television event, and it was also an early television appearance for Chris Berman, who would later become the iconic symbol of ESPN. Chris did local radio on a station in Naugatuck, a borough adjacent to Waterbury. He was partnered with Bob Sagendorf on a nightly program named *Calling All Sports*. Their pairing on 14NVR, WNVR, Naugatuck predated *Mike and the Mad Dog* on New York's WFAN and what would later become sports talk radio, one of the most successful radio formats of the last few decades.

Chris also did the morning traffic reports for that station. Often without leaving the parking lot of his condominium, he would report on traffic on I-84 and Route 8 with a confidence in its sameness that required no actual daily check-ins.

The telethon was a technical undertaking of a greater magnitude than channel 20 had attempted in the past. Would it work? Would live transmission fail us over the twenty hours? In the first year, everything went off without a hitch. However, my second—and last—telethon at the helm the next year was a different story. Just moments in, we lost our signal. When I approached the chief engineer for WATR-TV, Charlie Allen, his laconic response was "Last year we were lucky." A confidence-builder it was not.

The first year was magical. Guests arrived on time. Our host, Gail Janus, a popular weather forecaster on the Connecticut ABC affiliate who had moved on to a station in Atlanta, came back to give the broadcast a great deal of charm. The roll-ins of our services looked professional. The community got engaged. The Holiday Inn host, Mike Gaynor, was wonderful to work with as we converted their banquet room into a studio. WATR did a great job in rising to the challenge. Carmelita was all in, writing cue cards and taking on sundry responsibilities as needed.

I was so fortunate that this event left me with such a positive impression about the impact that television could have in mobilizing people for a good cause. It required a huge amount of planning and organization, but when all the elements came together, the fulfillment of a team effort was unmatched.

While radio strips away all the complexity and often leaves the performer alone, giving you great control, it enhances your individual vulnerability. Television envelopes you in a cocoon of professionals, each performing up to a standard lest the whole suffers significantly. Great pictures cannot overcome poor sound quality, and sloppy direction can take away from any performer's skillful on-air work.

I often think that video today has become so demystified as anyone with a smart phone can become a documentarian or dramatist. And channels do not program content as much as they vomit it up and encourage the viewer to find it in a sea of choices, which grow daily like weeds.

When television first appeared on my screen as a career option, the number of channel choices were relatively few, thus allowing a good result—even on a low-power UHF station. The telethon opened my eyes to the power and magnetic appeal of the medium as a force for good.

About the $40,000 goal that the national Easter Seals projected in the first year, we eclipsed it dramatically with the tote board screaming $130,000 by the end of the twenty hours!

Why then did I take a detour that might have made it such that I never found my way back to the obvious allure of television? It was a hunch that paid off as I was still in search of my life-defining role.

Chapter 9: AD-VISE

With as many outlets as I had at the time—my full-time job, my pursuit of a master's degree, and my part-time radio job—you might imagine that one more activity would have been a bridge too far.

In fact, in my mind, there was always the notion that a political career was in my future. I loved the game, knew that my personality was my greatest asset, had studied politics in college, and was working on the advanced degree in political communication. However, there has always been one part of the political game that I could not embrace. I am not a glad-hander who can pretend I want to be somewhere that I do not really want to be. I find that part of the game tedious and, frankly, disqualifying as a career path.

Dick Blumenthal, a Connecticut senator, loves that aspect of the game. There are two standard jokes about him: he will show up at a garage door opening if asked, and the other is to not get between him and a television camera as it can be the most dangerous place on earth at that moment. I must say that I didn't know him well when he was the longtime attorney general in our state, and yet when I later did a radio talk show, I discovered he was truly a kind man. To his credit, he would come to our studio for an interview with no notes and no aides. That was so rare. His answers could be oblique and gratuitous as when he agreed with one of my callers that there were good and bad parts of the energy bill and added, "I like the good parts and don't like the bad." That's it. He left it to the caller to imagine that they agreed on what parts those were.

I let this answer stand so that I could refer to it from time to time when politicians tried to evade questions. It was one of my set pieces, like the many crutches you develop when you are doing live broadcasts. Listen long enough and you can easily pick them up.

While I knew I would never put myself forward for political office, given my disdain for the niceties and insincerities, I still wanted to be part of the scramble in some way.

My friend Bob Zelinger and I started a part-time political consulting firm called AD-VISE. He was a great partner, and we enjoyed our foray into politics, creating the strategy and messaging for a few state legislative candidates. One of my classic campaign lines was "Good government starts with good people."

We left the battlefield of politics with a record of 2 and 0 as we helped State Sen. Louis Cutillo and State Rep. Maurice Mosley win several elections. We were personally very connected to Maurice, a black attorney in Waterbury who had great promise because of his winning personality and political acumen. He since went on to become a superior court judge. And while he would never hesitate to tell anyone in my company that we were the reason he won so handily, the truth is he would have won with or without us for a host of factors, not the least of which was that the district was a Democratic stronghold.

The company was a lark for two guys who knew that their futures would take them elsewhere but with the belief that this experience would be table setting in some fashion.

I still could not imagine that public service and having an impact on the politics of my community and state wasn't an itch that had to be scratched. What I had done in media, apart from AD-VISE, didn't speak to that, but I knew it was a yearning that had to be met.

I came out of an era when we believed in the possibility that government could be a force for good. John F. Kennedy and Camelot inspired an entire generation of us to pursue these kinds of dreams. I am blessed to have come of age in that moment. If I were coming of age today, I would be on the back side of forty years of a denigration of the public's trust in government, which has left America in the hands of people who never should have gotten into the field.

Since Watergate, the cynicism surrounding government has grown deeper and more toxic, owing to politicians currying favor and tilting the playing field toward private interests while at the same time diminishing the invaluable role that good public policy can have on a society. I am writing this look back in the age of the pandemic and bemoaning the lack of leadership that extended the time, cost, and suffering from the disease.

I also realize that I grew to become more of a political hobbyist whose lack of interest in the dull, often tedious aspects of politics is really where the impact is most felt. You must be in the trenches to make a difference, but I chose to "advise." Later in life I would use my role in media to make more of a difference—but always at arm's length without the grind-it-out aspects that define long-term success in making change. I tip my hat to those who have always been engaged and pursued the work despite the many hours involved and interactions with people with whom you might not otherwise choose to associate.

We were offered opportunities to run other campaigns. As relative neophytes in this game, we were picky about the candidates we worked for. I remember a local builder with zero political experience coming to us to run his campaign. He had no charisma and no compelling reason to run.

And I could tell he would have needed much hand-holding, which, in the end, would yield no results. He just didn't have it. Any political consultant must make that basic determination at the outset. There is nothing wrong with long odds or starting from behind, but the candidate must have some assets that you can market. He bored us to tears in our conversations. We turned down the assignment.

Another mayoral candidate, an attorney, requested a meeting at his lakeside home. Bob and I were greeted by his two German shepherds, one of whom took a nice bite out of Bob's leg. He went to the emergency room with the candidate hot in pursuit, more worried in Bob's estimation at the possibility of being sued than about Bob's health. We declined his invitation too.

While my work in politics was more an avocation than a career, it turned out to be important to me because I would use AD-VISE as a bridge to my true calling. You see, I left the Easter Seals Rehabilitation Center after four-plus years knowing it was time to move on.

I ended up in another place I did not belong, the Connecticut State Department of Education, as the spokesman for the department and assistant to the commissioner of education. I did not get a nudge from any of my political clients to get the position. I applied and was selected. To this day I do not really understand why, except that it became a big part of the plan. Do you believe in fate? If so, this falls neatly in that category. I will explain later.

I was from Waterbury, not a high-value location from which to impress a commissioner, who was Harvard educated and the former reform-minded superintendent of schools in Philadelphia. I had *no* background in the field, yet soon I would be writing his speeches and trying to explain arcane education policy to the Connecticut media. I can tell you this: if I had not graduated Phi Beta Kappa and had a master's degree by then, there was no way I would have gotten the position. Earlier, I alluded to the need to acquire extra education, certification, and credentials, just because it may open doors. This is what I meant.

So began a tumultuous two-year stint, which I would parlay into my life's work.

Chapter 10: Education

I was pleased to shake free of the grind of fundraising for a nonprofit to pursue an opportunity to write, think, and communicate about one of the most visible arms of state government—the agency overseeing public education. I must tell you that a forty-minute daily commute to Hartford to arrive at a bleak, sterile hulk of a state office building was not awe-inspiring.

While many of the people in our department were whip smart, primarily those handpicked by the commissioner as his assistants and chiefs of bureaus of the department, many lost souls patrolled the floor. Unfortunately, I inherited a few in my unit.

The first person whom I met each morning was a signal that Connecticut state government is populated by two different sets of characters, those who really believe in the mission of the agency and have great ambitions to serve and excel and those who are there to collect a paycheck and take the insular track to a nice pension. At the time state employment was a race to the ten-year mark to accrue incredible lifetime benefits afforded by strong union protections.

That person belonged to the latter category. He was the elevator operator. Oh, did I mention that the elevator had been automated a few years back? However, his job was never eliminated. His job was up and down, but the practice of featherbedding paid off well for him.

And the problem with state government is that the movers and shakers class relies on the other group to perform. And that's no easy task.

While I was in the commissioner's office as his assistant for communications, I managed my own band of dispossessed employees. Among them was a talented but hobbled former United Press International writer who ended up here after a bout with alcohol, a sweet woman named Lucy who walked around in an apron doing copies and Lord knows what else, a man named Ellery who basically clipped newspapers all day when there were any stories about education, and my secretary, Andrea. I couldn't quite determine why Andrea was there except that her parents wanted her out of the house and perhaps in pursuit of a spouse. Her energy level was low, and she seemed totally unimpressed that this young guy had come in to shake things up. She remained totally unshaken. It was with this crew that I went about the process of trying to meet the demanding expectations of Mark Shedd, commissioner of education.

Mark was a brilliant man who had his own struggles reforming the Philadelphia school system in the shadow of the city's strongman mayor, Frank Rizzo. Their battles were legendary. Mark was hired in Connecticut to awaken a state education department that for years played a slight role in policy and direction, leaving the hard work to the towns and cities. In fact, I got caught on that petard on day one. You see, as a reform-minded commissioner, he had just gotten a new funding mechanism for state schools through the legislature. The previous one was simply taking the number of students in each town and multiplying that figure by $250 per child. No math wizardry required to do that.

The new formula was understood by perhaps three people in the world, and none of them resided within the state's borders. It was based on a complicated formula of wealth, effort, and need per town. Wouldn't you know that on day one, I got a call from a local newspaper reporter asking me to explain the contours of the formula to him. Damned if I knew. It was not an auspicious start, but things got better.

Those in the commissioner's inner circle were an impressive group, and I raced to keep up. They went on to become commissioners of other agencies, majority leader of the State Senate, lieutenant governor, superintendents of schools in the state, and other important positions. These serious education types embraced me for my energy and were more than willing to fill up my basically empty head when it came to education policy and speak.

For some reason, the commissioner liked me, even though he would mark up my speeches like the best professors I had in college. Given his innate wisdom, I sensed that he knew I wasn't long for his world, but he still felt I could serve his purposes in the moment.

I developed an education news line for radio stations, public service announcements about education in the state, and a television series on major education issues, which aired on the state's PBS affiliate, Connecticut Public Television (CPTV).

The state operating grant that CPTV received each year came through the Department of Education. I used that bit of leverage to encourage CPTV to produce a monthly "roundtable on education" featuring Commissioner Shedd. He liked the publicity, and it gave me a chance to acquaint myself with the people at CPTV.

There was no love lost between Commissioner Shedd and Paul Taff, the president of CPTV at the time. Commissioner Shedd, for whatever reasons, did not hold Mr. Taff in high esteem, and he wasn't shy in expressing his feelings. When Mr. Taff later hired me to do his statewide network's public relations, Commissioner Shedd said it was the best move he had made.

Before that, there were some wrong moves made by the grants processing unit to correct. It was my job to address how the department made a $29 million funding error, which dogged the department and dragged down any of the initiatives the commissioner had begun. In my second year, I was always playing defense and catch-up. And that wasn't a position I liked to be in.

As it turned out, that day one question I got tripped up on by the reporter came back to haunt the entire agency. The grants processing unit at the department could not get it right either, and they included some federal funds in the complicated formula, thus inflating the amount of money that went out to the local districts.

It was the first dispiriting year of my professional life. On the cusp of thirty years of age, I knew I had to walk away from this position. I never became enmeshed in the concept that public education was the hill I wanted to die on as it was for so many professionals who worked there. I gave it a good try and somehow made enough of an impression on others in the field that I was asked by the national superintendents' group to run the press room for their national conference in New Orleans at the Superdome for two consecutive years.

In fact, I organized the first news conference for Terrel Bell, the first-ever US secretary of education, at one of those confabs. And one thing I did while employed there came back to give me some real joy almost forty years later.

I was moderating a panel on "fake news" for teachers on behalf of the Connecticut Humanities Council in 2018. A recent teacher of the year came up to me and thanked me for initiating the Teacher of the Year program in Connecticut. I gave him a puzzled look, and he shared an email from Garrett Stack, a public relations professional from a local school district in my day, who remembered (I didn't) that I had brought the idea back to the commissioner after a national conference. After seeing a presentation from the sponsor, Encyclopedia Britannica, I urged him to sign on, and the state has been involved to this day.

The Connecticut Teacher of the Year Council invited me to be their guest of honor at the annual awards ceremony that year to be recognized for reviving the program in Connecticut. In remarks at that event, I said, "As someone who comes from an industry (media) prone to draw undue attention to itself and be self-congratulatory, I can observe that your industry—teaching and learning—garners too little attention and appreciation for satisfying audiences much tougher than ours—parents and students—entrusting their most precious gifts and futures to you."

In this moment of school disequilibrium brought on by the pandemic, those words come rushing back, reminding me of their simple, incontrovertible truth.

Chapter 11: Home Again

I decided that my stint in public policy was just about to come to an end. I could put the guaranteed tax base funding formula behind me, and I would never again have to see an apron-clad Lucy running through the department like Edith Bunker on amphetamines nor would I have to approach that soulless building on a beautiful day knowing I would be in its antiseptic environment until night.

But not before I left with a big bang. It was somebody's idea, not mine, to send me off with a roast. It was hardly a laugh-filled environment, to say the least. The roast proved to be a first and a last for the Connecticut Department of Education under this commissioner. After some ribald jokes, the commissioner, a staid and steady man of Maine, said, "Let's not do this again."

To his credit, Mark Shedd was one of the most decent and admirable people I have ever worked for. He was stubbornly committed to the work of bringing Connecticut's school policy into the modern era. His dedication was most visible when he invited staff members to brief him as he underwent hours-long blood transfusions for a form of leukemia, which ultimately took his life.

So I was done there but really had no landing pad in mind. I realize it was a risky move in an era when the concept of freelance work was not as common as it is in today's gig economy. Yet I knew I had to make a turn and didn't ponder the impact it might have on getting back into an organization down the road. I just did it. Fortunately, I had the AD-VISE shingle still available to me, though my partner was now ensconced in full-time work and law school. I was truly on my own.

I realized that I enjoyed the pursuit of business more than I did the actual capture. It was exhilarating to make the proposal yet daunting to realize that the more fanciful the idea, the more work it would be to carry out.

I moved into the basement of our first, very modest home, surrounded by a woodstove, a ping-pong table, and a backdrop of a Pepsi-Cola wall montage left over from the home's first occupant. Imagine if I were asked to do a Cisco Webex in this pandemic era with that set piece behind me. That would not have conveyed gravitas.

I declared the business as one that did public relations and advertising consulting and proclaimed, "It's not all glitter. It's tough work getting your message across. But now in Waterbury, there is professional help."

So began a nearly one-year odyssey, an exodus of sorts, from the comforts of having staff (even if they were dysfunctional), sharing office banter and interaction, and being part of something larger than yourself. I had other professionals I would turn to for services such as graphic design, but it was just me in my basement.

As I look back, that should have been a terrifying thought. Would any business come my way? Could I make a living in this rather small community? Had my stepping away affected my life's chances going forward? Would I fail, and if so, then what?

Fortunately another Easter Seals Center, a larger one in New Haven, wanted to do a telethon on the state's ABC affiliate, so they hired me as their chief advisor on the project, given my experience in Waterbury. A consultant so soon? Strike my earlier reflections on consultancies.

Other small businesses were looking for advertising help. Lessack's Weight Loss Center was owned by an old high school beau of my sister. Paul Lessack was an interesting guy, an aggressive self-promoter who would take it upon himself to go to the local newspaper and replace a beautifully designed ad with an unreadable one set in one-point type, revealing every credential he had earned since preschool.

And another client, a nonprofit thirty miles southwest of home, wanted me to spend at least one day a week at their facility. I felt like a real fish out of water as I settled in for a day with little direction or motivation to perform.

On the horizon, however, was a big proposal to do the advertising for a local chain called the Pie Plate. The ideas I developed and the proposal I drew up, to me, were sure to win the business. They didn't. I was crestfallen. I don't recall panicking, but that would have been my normal default position.

My wife, Carmelita, was pregnant with our first child, Wade, and planned to step away from her job as a physical therapist for a bit, all the while selling Mary Kay Cosmetics products. While she did well, as always, a pink Cadillac was not found outside our ranch home on the east side of Waterbury.

I was at a crossroads well ahead of when I ever imagined or wanted to get there. Just at that moment, I learned that there was an opening at CPTV for someone to head up its public relations for the statewide public broadcasting network.

I had developed a good relationship with Sharon Blair, the TV programming chief who also oversaw the public relations department. She was the person who green-lighted the commissioner's monthly program on CPTV. I think she imagined that anyone able to convince her to air that boring talkfest could be effective doing public relations for the statewide network.

Fortunately, after a summer of discontent and nervousness about my next move, I was offered the position and started one week before Wade was born. Little did I know that it would be my professional home through a period that saw both our children grow up and leave the house. I didn't plan to stay, but I had too much fun to go. And so my life's most fulfilling work truly began here. It proved to be the ride of a lifetime.

Chapter 12: Public Broadcasting

In truth, and for the first time, I will admit that when I started in the public television business, I knew little about the programming. After all, it was a curious programming service. It invited tiny tots to watch great educational programs such as *Sesame Street, Mister Rogers,* and *The Electric Company.* Then it said goodbye to those viewers until they had grown into responsible adults who liked classical music and good British drama (and had a few dollars to contribute to the service). In most cases the lag between the two was thirty years or more. And I was still in that in-between age group.

What I did know was that there was a certain cache and prestige associated with the service, and I liked that. It was akin to working at the state's education department as opposed to, say, the motor vehicle unit. Both were state agencies, but their status was different in terms of value to society.

Thinking back, I was just grateful to be back in a professional working environment. I was fortunate that a lifeline back to a more conventional working environment had been established with the folks at CPTV before I left the education department. I just needed to find the right opening.

That opportunity occurred almost a year after leaving the department.

In connection with my self-appointed exile to the basement, I should caution that such risks are all right to take, but do not be surprised if the road back to a conventional setting is longer and tougher than you realized.

When my twenty-seven-year stay at CPTV ended, my persona and my institution were indelibly linked. I had become literally the face of what CPTV represented to the community for most of that period.

Twice after leaving the station, I was asked to come back, but I realized that my moment in time had come and gone. I left little undone and with no regrets. The last thing I wanted to do was attempt to surpass the things we had accomplished. I knew the times were not right to do that in 2009, and I wanted to leave with the legacy unblemished. How many old ballplayers stay on a few too many years? Do you remember Willie Mays as a Met or Michael Jordan as a Wizard?

I went there to develop greater visibility for CPTV and quickly realized that many of the good feelings surrounding the institution were leased from the national programming that emanated from our transmitters and derived from the imaginations of other PBS stations. Our creation of that content was spotty in that moment. However, that was not my job. I had to stay in my own lane and create good impressions for what we were doing, even if I knew more was possible.

I still had much to learn about public television. I performed to my fullest the duties assigned and waited for a larger portfolio to present itself.

My position as head of public relations and on-air promotion allowed me to make a favorable impression from the start with Jerry Franklin, the incoming president of the company. The incumbent in the position was Paul Taff. He was a nice man who seemed a bit disengaged to a newcomer like me. He had settled in for a long stay, as many public television executives do, and had a nice gig. His curmudgeonly style worked for the board of trustees—until it did not.

While fundraising is the lifeblood of an operation like public broadcasting, Mr. Taff had little interest in it. His background was as an executive at WQED in Pittsburgh, and Fred Rogers's program was in his portfolio. Lunch is prime time for fundraising calls, mind you, in the schedule of most nonprofit executives. He would go out to lunch alone every day at the same spot. And he would open every piece of mail not addressed specifically to someone at the station. He also was famous for the quick thrust as represented in a note to then programming chief, Sharon Blair, to the effect, "Paul Newman lives in Connecticut—get him." Whatever that means. He did not specify dead or alive. The first hint of snow would send Mr. Taff to the exits.

I tell you this not to disparage the man because we got along well then and when he later became president of the Connecticut Broadcasters Association. Rather I want to set the scene that would later be described as "Sleepy TV" by the man who succeeded Mr. Taff and gave me my new, expanded marching orders.

I was not unfulfilled in my duties leading the public relations effort for the station. While I was sure there was more that we could be doing to serve the community, I was still trying to understand how this byzantine system worked. There was a maxim in public television that went something like this: "It's not remarkable that we get in a circle and fire at each other, but it is surprising how quickly we can reload."

I would later write in the system's trade publication how fractured and dysfunctional the system was from my standpoint, but while being a critic, I also become a player who learned the rules and how to benefit from them. The two roles, practitioner and critic, seemed to be at odds. However, recognizing that change is hard, you carry on.

There were a few notable aspects to my three-plus years in the public relations realm. I used them to get a better take on how the station and the system worked, and I honed a skill that would become a calling card throughout my long stay.

As required working in a nonprofit organization, I volunteered for a function that had become so important to public broadcasting's survival—on-air pledge drive hosting. At first it was a lark. People knew that I had a background in radio, had produced telethons, and did cable service launches and election coverage for my cousin Harold Kramer, who headed Valley Cable in the Naugatuck Valley, Seymour. If there were a split screen, one moment I would be offering up HBO and the next *Masterpiece Theatre*.

There were more experienced people at CPTV who had done this for years, but quickly I became one of the key on-air presenters. I had great energy and passion in my presentation and over the years took delight in trying to hone a psychological message meant to separate a viewer from some of the money in his or her wallet. It was one of the few unscripted, extemporaneous opportunities in television to tell a story, make a case, and see the results happen in real time. That is an adrenaline rush.

While public speaking is often number one on people's list of fears, to me, it was second nature. It was Dad's gift. Above all others, it made me something of an indispensable commodity during my long stay. It was also part of that competitiveness in me. As new staff members and volunteers came into the fold, I was determined to surpass their totals for this or that program.

If you think you can explain Big Bird's value to kids better than me, try this.

I began to want the choice assignments, moving from daytime to prime time. And when special guests such as Yanni, John Tesh, and Michael Crawford, the original "Phantom," joined us, I wanted to be the one who interviewed them. And nine times out of ten, I was.

An eight-hour-a-day job, by virtue of this, turned into an all-encompassing way of life. And the hours became open-ended during various times of year.

While I liked the association with public television and its aura, it was a real bonus becoming a statewide media personality. It was never part of the plan, assuming there was a plan in the first place.

The board decided that Mr. Taff's diffident style was not what would drive CPTV into the future. To the north, they saw a dynamic young executive at a small PBS station in Springfield, Massachusetts, who was a flashy on-air presenter and exuded an impressive level of confidence in his own abilities when contrasted with our own leadership. They recruited Jerry Franklin to succeed Mr. Taff, and that opened an array of opportunities for me.

He wanted me, as "his" new PR guy, to come to his send-off at his former station to see how people responded to him. His ego and drive were on full display. Jerry Franklin was a man in a hurry. As my longtime assistant, Lisa Di Donato Cambria, would say, he was like "a fart in a spacesuit." Since I was one of the first to meet and get to know him, the impression I made would signal my future chances there.

He had an impression that CPTV was undervalued and little appreciated and that we had a lot of work to do, thus the appellation "Sleepy TV." While that may have been true at this express moment in time, this characterization did not square with CPTV's many programming contributions of the past. In fact, CPTV's first president, Ben Huddleston, had worked at WNBC-TV in New York and surrounded himself with a strong team of professionals.

CPTV first went on the air at 9:40 a.m. on October 1, 1962, when then WEDH became one of only three educational television stations in New England. In the beginning, it was housed in the basement of the library at Trinity College in the south end of Hartford and then set up shop in Boardman Hall.

I was told that on cold nights, the steampipes could be so loud that you could not hear the broadcasts. The technical equipment was bulky and cumbersome and would become more unsuitable over time as the pace of broadcasting quickened.

CPTV's engineering wizard, Jack Kean, hired away from WGBH in Boston, designed what is said to be the first handheld camera ever built in America. He took an old RCA color camera, gutted it, and put it back together in a way that the camera operator only had the tubes and the lens. The electronics were stored in a backpack that another person wore. Once its cameras were made nimble for mobile production, local programming possibilities expanded too.

CPTV's most celebrated effort was *Mundo Real*, the first television series to star a Puerto Rican family and to be broadcast in both Spanish and English. Another strong entry, *Lookin' Better*, which Jay Whitsett created, was designed to show how minorities overcame obstacles. There was an emphasis on women of color, and the first guest was Rachel Robinson, Jackie Robinson's wife.

Episodes of *Theater in America* and *American Playhouse* were done in Hartford although they were WNET, New York series. CPTV was close by, capable, and a cheaper venue than midtown Manhattan. Notables such as a young Meryl Streep starred there in *Uncommon Women and Others*, and others performing in CPTV's studios included Richard Thomas, Swoosie Kurtz, and Jeff Daniels in Sam Shepard's *Fifth of July*.

From the beginning, CPTV differed from most such entities as it was not owned or operated by a state agency of a university system. It was on its own and had to find creative ways to survive without a sponsoring agency.

To earn the support of state government while not being licensed to it, CPTV became a window into state government with many programs focused on the government of the state, the least-covered level of government as people were more caught up in the politics of their town or city and the federal government.

Programs such as *The Fourth Estate*, led by Hartford attorney Joseph Steinberg, delved into the hottest issues in Connecticut weekly. Bob Douglas, a mainstay, hosted *The People's Caucus*, an hour-long interview and call-in show. CPTV also did much coverage of elections in the state, including gavel-to-gavel coverage of important hearings and the state's political conventions, and the station made a bold statement in 1982, just as I arrived, when it hosted a series of six debates between Sen. Lowell Weicker and his fiery challenger, Rep. Toby Moffett.

Had I actually been a more critical cog when Jerry Franklin arrived with line responsibility for, say, programming, he would have circled back and laid blame at my doorstep for not getting more things done in the mid-1980s. He was not a man to linger in the past. He made quick assessments of what he saw in the moment and believed he would be able to improve upon those results.

He saw me as an aggressive PR guy who just did not have much to work with. The old saying is that PR is "doing good and letting people know about it." The first part, *the doing*, is critical. He was determined to change that. To his credit, and I will never quite understand it, he did not see me as a threat. He was confident and competitive. Did he really want to have one of his sidekicks be the face of the station when that should fall to him?

He quickly realized that I had one thing he needed—a real understanding of the state of Connecticut. Jerry had moved coast-to-coast in pursuit of his career and had been in the military. I was a Connecticut kid most of my life; I came from an earthy city and had professional associations from my time in state government, which were useful to him. And I knew folks throughout media in Connecticut, as he could tell in promoting him, and he appreciated that.

While he would move people in and out of positions with little regard for its impact on them, I became something of a confidant. I, too, was in a hurry, but my approach was to walk around people and not to knock them over.

Although different in style, we built a symbiotic relationship over a quarter century that was highly productive for the station. Often Jerry would make a big pronouncement, a bold play not tethered to much of substance, and he would look to me to make it work.

Even though every other manager with major responsibility at the station while I was there was, at some point, demoted, moved aside, swept under in a reorganization, or simply removed, I was continually given more responsibilities until I decided to strip back my portfolio.

Looking back, I am amazed that we coexisted for that length of time as other departments were tossed about many times over. My department and responsibilities were left unscathed in one bloodletting or another. I often felt survivor's remorse as one department head or another experienced a decimation of their group, and my group would be left untouched.

At this point you must be imagining that I was an enabler or a provocateur within the company, somehow abetting the process. While lacking any objectivity in describing my role, I think my insulation from the raucous vicissitudes of the boss had more to do with how my responsibilities were carried out and the distinction it brought to the company and its external audiences. Perhaps in making the product look so good, we helped hide the internal confusion. Jerry's genius was in knowing that so long as the outward face shone bright, the internal upheavals would be tolerated by the board.

I was never a political infighter anywhere I worked. I preferred to go about my business and insulate my employees through our efforts. In hindsight I was self-involved in that regard. I was unhappy about the ongoing disruption, but its impact directly on my work was marginal, so I kept in my lane. It can be a tough call. Do you jeopardize what you are achieving to help put out fires elsewhere?

Having seen as much as I did, perhaps I just became inured to it, or I valued more the opportunity to create my own reality rather than trying to change what others were facing.

In 1986, a little over a year after Jerry took the helm, I assumed responsibility for developing statewide content as the manager for programming of a five-channel network. It was a promotion I never sought or expected and frankly one over which I questioned my preparedness to assume.

Jerry Franklin gave me the keys to a car that in his view was parked in the garage and said, "If this thing starts, take it where you want. Create programs that make a difference in this community and get people's attention."

So why, you might ask, was I exempt from the flashpoints and constant rearrangements at the station? I have come to believe that while Jerry thought he was the best fundraiser in the building, despite the high level of quality talent he hired to oversee that effort over the years, he grew to respect my instincts, as much as if not more so than his own, when it came to programming. At the very least, he felt my knowledge of Connecticut and my deft ability to make programming deals beneficial to the station were worthy of support.

Jerry's determination to gain dominion over what had previously been a station run largely by the engineering department was critical to my success. While their innovations were at one point crucial to the station's development, the top of the heap status was becoming a hindrance to getting programming accomplished.

My long tenure as programming chief, and the various titles and responsibilities that followed, had just begun, and I had some proving to do—to him and myself.

Chapter 13: Programmer in Charge

There I was, in another place I did not belong.
While I had made friends at the station, I do not think too many folks imagined that I would be dictating programming decisions instead of public relations strategies. It is amazing how much a title or responsibility shift changes perceptions. Who, him? Why? It was a good question in my case. It was not like I was coming in from another station or had been next in line.

Sharon Blair, my predecessor in the post, had additional responsibilities on her plate. She not only oversaw the programming for the network out of Hartford, but she was also assigned to manage a separate schedule for WEDW channel 49 in Fairfield County and try to lure national productions to CPTV.

I took a piece of her portfolio, so she could concentrate on the others. In many ways Sharon was responsible for Jerry Franklin being hired at CPTV. By trying, in vain, to lure Fairfield County viewers away from WNET out of New York, she time-shifted and delayed many of the showcase PBS prime-time programs on the entire network. Our ratings in the

Hartford-New Haven market tumbled, and board members took note of what Jerry's former station in Springfield was doing. In fact, all they were doing was "riding the bird," as it is called in the industry, airing programs as they were being offered. That and his obvious energy, as opposed to that of our leader, drew enough of a contrast to interest them in poaching him.

Looking back on this moment, I really did not know what I was going to do to build programs people would watch and talk about. I knew the market and had a feel for what was promotable, but I had never done it before. How do you marshal resources to mount a production? Who can produce material that really tells stories?

It was my naivete that unshackled me enough not to be limited by history or organizational structure. I built my own reality just as I was able to do at the rehabilitation center. I built a new model using contract producers to augment our capacity, helping them build content specialties and drawing on their expertise time and again. While there were talented people on staff, they were too few in number for the ambitions I came to exhibit. Today that is the norm for many industries. I built my version of the gig economy in a rather stodgy environment.

Fortunately, I had a talented producer/director and production whiz—and to this day a good friend—Jay Whitsett, who became my production manager and went along for the wild ride upon which we were about to embark.

I know that he and many others had doubts about the types of new talent I brought into the mix. After all, many of them had no production experience. They were writers, teachers, and theater people, an eclectic blend of new recruits. My thought was that their storytelling capacity was harder to teach than the production aspects of the job. Jay was there to guide them in this evolution. We had talented camera operators who all thought they could create better visuals than a producer and were all too willing to show the newcomers the ropes if they thought the program had merit. In almost any television environment, the group that needs to be convinced that something of value is happening is the crew. They are often disgruntled because they have, for years, taken direction from people whom they thought were lazy or uninspired on projects that they found less than scintillating.

To make it worse, I myself had no production experience other than the two telethons. I was not schooled in various elements of production, such as budgeting or directing. I was a big-picture editorialist. I am not certain if it is even a definable skill set. I just had great confidence that, given the time and resources, my judgments about content would pave the way to success.

I still do not know how that confidence overcame all the limitations I thought I brought to the job, never having gone to Syracuse as Jay did with its great communications program or Emerson in Boston as my future production manager, Haig Papasian. I got accepted but chose not to attend.

I must have been aware that, despite his impulsiveness, Jerry had a hunch about me. Rest assured that if I did not start making some moves quickly to imbue faith in him about his curious choice, my tenure could have been short-lived.

The most important thing I did was open the door to CPTV—literally. In the past many had considered the station a closed shop, not open to new ideas or new people. I reversed that. In so doing I built relationships that both benefited the station and enhanced my life. I will devote the next chapter to one of those people as an illustration.

I also built new partnerships with a polling agency to develop programming around "Connecticut Viewpoint," a survey to ascertain what our state's residents cared about. Once we determined what was on their minds, we designed programs related to those subjects.

Furthermore, I reached out to the Connecticut Humanities Council and, with its dynamic and brilliant leader, Bruce Fraser, developed a series based on PBS's *American Experience* called *The Connecticut Experience*.

We did rich, intellectually rigorous yet entertaining documentaries such as *The Roots of Roe*, which was about our state's central importance to reproductive rights in America, and *Between Boston and New York*, tackling the perennial question—what is the true essence of Connecticut? If you think of cowboys in Texas or lobsters in Maine, what symbolizes our state? Try it. It is not easy.

I wanted us to get gritty and weigh in on controversy, so we did a program titled *Connecticut's Death Row*, and our producer, Sean Shay, gleaned the exit interview with Michael Ross, the last person to be executed in Connecticut before the death penalty was abolished. I commissioned him to do a similar treatment in *Connecticut's Drug Web*.

We took on the long-simmering strike affecting Colt Industries in a coproduction with an outside company, Motion Inc., and producer Anita Coles examined changes to the welfare system and its impact on Connecticut.

And while CPTV had always been a good public affairs shop, doing live debates and convention coverage as well as coverage of the legislature, we added new signatures, such as *The Next Governor*, a documentary series on each election cycle.

Aware that our viewers were sensitive to environmental issues, I developed an unusual partnership with the Connecticut State Department of Environmental Protection to do a series of documentaries on the closing of town dumps, river management in the state, Long Island Sound, and hunting. We maintained editorial control as I was a purist about such things, and that agreement was tested on the hunting documentary, which they made clear they were not happy with. I know the title "Blood Sports" was not to their liking. It ran anyway.

I was keen to see what national PBS programming mattered to our audience and mirror it in statewide content. We would strive for quality, to meet audience expectations, to the degree that our budgets would allow.

We did many history programs about significant people, institutions, and events in Connecticut such as Mark Twain, Samuel Colt, the USS *Nautilus*, and the Wadsworth Atheneum and flooded the state with nostalgia programs, overseen by Andrea Hanson and produced by the talented Rich Hanley. *The Flood of '55*, *When Disaster Struck Connecticut*, and *Remember When* became staples during our on-air fundraising campaigns.

It is fair to say that I put the pedal on the gas, and CPTV became a resonant producer of content that got Connecticut's attention.

The secret was developing long-form programming, which commercial stations did not do, and understanding the national strands of PBS programming, which we could replicate on a statewide basis. We had ten or more documentary projects going at the same time and often ran edit shifts around the clock.

At this point, it is worth noting that while my emphasis was on state-based productions, PBS is a service, not a network. By charter, PBS cannot produce programs. This anachronism goes back to the turn of the National Educational Network into PBS. WNET in New York and WGBH in Boston had staked out their positions as the production centers for public television and were reluctant to give up those positions to this new entity.

In effect, this meant that all local stations could become national producers from remote corners of the country. And while this accounted for some of the richness and quirkiness of public television programming, it clearly became a difficult model to sustain with the advent of cable television. More on that later.

You might imagine that some of my state-based programs could be attractive to national audiences because the content was relevant to people throughout the country, and there were distribution outlets, such as Eastern Educational Television Network and, later, American Public Television (APT), that could send them out to the other stations and glean larger audiences. While you could run a program by PBS, they were the toughest distribution avenue to go down. Their standards were higher, and the demand for their schedule was greater.

Having said that, early on the state programming unit did make a play to PBS on a few shows. *Roots of Roe* was nationally distributed by PBS, even gaining a good review in the *New York Times*. Congratulations to producer Andrea Haas Hubbell on that.

In the period that I am writing about, Sharon Blair still maintained responsibility for national programming. My duties were focused on what we presented locally to our Connecticut audience. I was responsible for how we built a schedule attractive to Connecticut with PBS programs, acquisitions, and our own productions. Andrea Hanson, who had direct responsibility for the broadcast schedule, was an experienced and capable partner who had great knowledge and sensitivity to our audiences. Her long history at CPTV helped curb my more "commercial" tendencies in some of the acquisitions we made. Did we really need a ten-part series on the history of the mob in New York? The competitive side of me said yes, and we would have great back-and-forth debates about such choices.

I was never shy about jumping on to a curiosity, shall we say, as I did in deciding to broadcast a basketball game between the University of Bridgeport and Sacred Heart University because it featured the otherworldly seven-foot-seven-inch Manute Bol. He was getting much national attention at the time. I recall doing a pledge break from midcourt at halftime. I do not recall if our version of the long and the short of it (seven feet, seven inches versus five feet, six inches) ever shared the same frame, but I have been known to stand on what is called an apple box to allow for these images to coexist without me talking to the other person's navel.

In the end, I became more sensitive to the public television audience, and Andrea became more confident in my judgment on how far we could go.

As I became introduced to nearby programmers in influential markets such as New York, Boston, and Philadelphia, clearly their openness to this neophyte was based on their respect for Andrea Hanson. If he was all right for her, then he must be all right with us. I traded on the goodwill she had developed over many years.

While Sharon's style was more laissez-faire and never threatened by this upstart she was responsible for bringing into the shop, I kept looking to produce programs that might satisfy our Connecticut audiences as a first consideration *and* might travel beyond our borders.

The Connecticut unit became a de facto New England unit, recognizing the appeal of shows such as *Islands of New England, Cape Cod Reflections, Lighthouses of New England,* and *Vampires of New England* both in our state and in far-flung places like San Francisco. You get the picture. We distributed those through what is now APT in Boston. I secured funding from APT to produce them.

In my own way, I justified calling them Connecticut programs because they were topics our audience wanted to see, and, well, no one else was doing them. In this way, and with other Connecticut-centric programs, my reputation for good, watchable television began to grow throughout the system.

And while I was picking up a lot of information about the system and how it works, attending national meetings and promoting what we were aggressively offering, my focus was still ostensibly local. However, these forays into the national arena whet my appetite for producing programs more people would see. One such program was *Thumbs Across America,* with its remarkable mastermind, Andrew P. Jones.

Chapter 14: Andrew P. Jones

Throughout Andrew P. Jones's remarkable lifetime, he visited many hot spots throughout the globe, capturing lives caught up in turmoil. It was a subject he knew all too well.

As a child of the projects of Richmond, Virginia, he became the exception at every turn, going to an exclusive boarding high school in New England and on to a musical conservatory in Boston. He was smart, clever, talented, and fearless. And we developed an unlikely friendship.

As an African American activist woke before that word had any connotation, he could see inauthenticity a mile away. His antennae went above the highest peak, looking to call out the many people he had encountered over the years who could not understand how this man with the 1960s Afro and disheveled look could be as honest and direct in his communication, never mincing words and exuding confidence in his estimable abilities.

When my phone rang and it was him calling from Boston, I didn't know what he was expecting from me. I imagined he had his wires crossed and thought he was talking to just another programmer whose job was meant to block his path. Instead, he found a level of receptivity and respect that was genuine and became a hallmark of our relationship.

As indicated, I was open to many producers, and new voices, along the road in this grand experiment to multiply our impact in the community and bring creativity to CPTV. Each had a special gift. Mine was to encourage them to bring us their best work. And while they all left a mark on me, none would quite like Andrew.

In that first call, he stroked me and said that the word in Boston was that CPTV was an open shop and invited creative ideas and independent producers. I was thrilled that this reputation was seeping out and bringing talented people to our doorstep.

His idea was to showcase himself not only as a producer but also as a great personality in front of the camera, trying to hitchhike across America to see what the country was really like. Who are the people who would help him along his journey? He said all he needed was $2,500 and edit time. After asking a bit more about his background as a stringer for ABC in Boston, I agreed.

By the end of the call, an incredible documentary, *Thumbs Across America*, was born and, more importantly, a friendship until his tragic passing. *Thumbs Across America* was obviously not a local program, and that was still my beat, but I was getting ambitious and blurring lines.

As you can imagine, it was not easygoing for Andrew. He was about to give up in Pennsylvania as hours passed with no ride. I came to learn that it took a lot to dampen his spirit and creative vision. The documentary, available on YouTube, took some unexpected turns, particularly when he got picked up by a young mom and her child in the South. He was even surprised at the way he was helped along the path by a cast of unlikely American characters. He made it, barely, to San Francisco, and the production was an early light cam masterpiece.

Andrew was a restless soul. His energy and ideas were boundless. He would call me from remote places like Panama during the American incursion there as he shot his image in a mirror to document what he had just seen or from Vietnam as he was running down the story of children of American soldiers left behind and reviled in a country as another unwanted reminder of "the American war." His call came through in the middle of the night as he wrestled with a bout of malaria.

I had courage in supporting many of his projects, but his daring was not in my lexicon. I marveled at the spirit and courage of the man.

Years later Andrew moved to South Africa to help disabled young people learn the art of documentary productions. There, he and his soon-to-be wife, Kubeshi, met and had a family. Several years after he moved to South Africa, I reacquainted with Andrew. I was there to produce a musical special called *Ipi N'tombi*, the South African *Porgy and Bess* for PBS. I commissioned Andrew to do a backstage look at the production, which we could offer to PBS stations.

Much time had passed, but my respect for Andrew continued unabated. Years later, when I returned to radio full time, he was a guest on one of my first programs, promoting a book he had penned on Barack Obama.

It was with deep sadness that I later learned of a marital altercation in which he attempted to harm his wife and later took his own life. Many deaths I grieve. His I mourned. A few years ago, with great pride, my daughter, Leora, who is active in social justice causes in Boston, helped me organize a tribute to Andrew.

In addition to being a talented producer, he was a classically trained violinist and community organizer. His temerity was always on display. When a customs official at an airport challenged Andrew to prove he owned the violin he was carrying, he made one request—that the customs official remove the violin from the case and hand it to him. He went on to play a concerto from one of the masters and, of course, was allowed through.

Back in the 1980s, he and his partner in the effort, Curtis Davis, who later helped design the Smithsonian National Museum of African American History & Culture, tried to politically subdivide portions of Boston from downtown. Their vision was a Roxbury, Dorchester, Mattapan, and Jamaica Plain area called Mandela. They envisioned self-rule in the truest sense. Their efforts put the breakaway proposal on the ballot twice, and while they lost, it is a classic example of self-determination. Much has been written about their noble failure—if you want to call it that. In an era of social media, I have no doubt that Andrew, a great polemicist, would have pushed it through. He never got another chance.

The tribute to Andrew in the heart of what would have been "Mandela" was my way of honoring the most unique person I met along my professional road. I am close to tears as I use these pages to once again remember Andrew P. Jones. He touched me so profoundly by sharing once that I was the only white television executive he ever trusted. I was honored to lay witness to his brilliance. His star had to burn out early. It was too hot to survive the injustices that tore at him from deep within.

RIP, APJ.

Chapter 15: 1989

CPTV had been a tinker's dream.

As a UHF television network, it was a jerry-rigged labyrinth of transmitters, relays, microwave setups, and a corps of engineers who often had to work on a shoestring to keep the various channels connected and functioning. It was a complicated business.

Since the general manager of a television station rarely has great technical skills, they can be bamboozled by the chief engineer to keep providing resources to their area "if you want to stay on the air."

I would imagine most public television stations that cobble together budgets with an unpredictable mix of state grants, viewer dollars, corporate kindness, and a dash of federal support often take shortcuts in assembling their delivery systems. I cannot tell you how many budget meetings would end with our chief engineer saying, "You know, we should have a klystron in the budget. It could go at any time." I had no idea what a klystron was, nor did anyone else in the room. To get this book into the educational category at a library, I have since researched that it is a specialized linear-beam vacuum tube, invented in 1937, which is used as an amplifier for high radio frequencies, from UHF up into the microwave range. It is also used as output tubes in UHF television transmitters.

Jack Kean, the longtime vice president for engineering at CPTV, was a very smart man, and he would let you know it simply by giving you that stare and pause as he explained why some programming feat we tried to pull off was near impossible given our capabilities. "A live shot with five cameras from where?" His innovation in developing a more transportable camera setup was vital to what I had planned. I do recall that when I started in programming, we would often go out on shoots with an engineer and one-inch or two-inch tape machines. It was a cumbersome setup and not one conducive to getting a lot of projects done.

I recently interviewed Marc Randolph, a cofounder of Netflix, for my podcast, and it was remarkable how technology played into its development. Had the technology not advanced from VHS to DVD, the shipping costs would have been prohibitive, and the little red box would never become the transition to streaming. And streaming would have never become possible without advances in the cost and reliability of bandwidth. While you do not want the technology to drive the bus, clearly it facilitates what you can do.

Jerry Franklin was determined to wrest control from "can't-be-done engineers" to help foster the go-go shop he, too, envisioned. In me, he had the right partner. I was not married to the past and had little knowledge of the tools. What I did know is that we had stories to share, and I wanted to have the editorial side of the shop in control with new approaches to production and new talents to imbue the culture with a sense of possibility.

One by one these people found their way into CPTV. I was the orchestrator and Jay Whitsett the facilitator. In recent exchanges on this era, Jay recalls the buzz at one leadership retreat after he and I overwhelmed the system, and as one retreat leader said, "The place is run by Larry and Jay." Jay Whitsett was critical to so much of what we did to put a defining stamp on CPTV. Why then, later in our tenure, would I play a cruel practical joke on someone I cared so much about?

Joe Consentino, a successful producer from Ridgefield, Connecticut, had a relationship with Chet Forte, the fabled director of ABC's *Monday Night Football*. He was considered the pioneer of many of the techniques still employed to make live sports so compelling. He upended norms for camera angles and graphics usage. He was the man who developed the intimate coverage style that still defines coverage of the NFL. Despite his brilliance and long tenure, Forte was down on his luck having admitted that he had a gambling problem. He bet on every game he directed.

Consentino thought this would be a great subject for a *Frontline* documentary on PBS. I agreed, so the two came to the station to discuss. When I told Jay, himself a fine director, that Chet Forte would be here, he said he had to meet this pioneer and directing icon.

I brought Chet into the studio as Jay was involved in a production and made proper introduction. Chet, as I prepped him, said, "Jay Whitsett, Jay Whitsett, did you direct *The World Is Jazz?*" Jay was dumbstruck that his idol knew of his work.

Excitedly Jay said, "Yes."

Chet, as prompted, said, "That was a piece of shit."

Jay was mortified. Joke delivered. Finally, laughs all around. Sorry, Jay, it was too good to pass up.

Jerry was big on leadership retreats and the appearance of a team strategy. Large pieces of paper with magic markers were meant to scribe great thoughts about the future of the institution and how CPTV could be a leader in the industry. The truth was that the board wanted Jerry to hold these confabs, and we would come back, transcribe, and forget what was said there.

I remember one in a lovely bucolic setting at Rye Brook, New York, in Westchester County. One of the team building exercises was to fall back into your colleagues' arms. I distinctly remember looking at the two who were assigned to have my back and not trusting one of them not to let me fall violently to the ground. I survived that episode but knew that as a disruptor who threw away all the previous playbooks, I better produce some tangible evidence that the combination of energy, instinct, and naivete was, at some point, going to pay off.

When I took over the programming duties in 1986, CPTV had never made a big splash in amassing Emmy Awards in the region. Our region happened to be, in the minds of many, the premier local television market in the country, encompassing the Boston/New England region. It was said at the time that WCVB in Boston was the best producer of local programming in the country. In fact, they were known for developing local drama from time to time, which was almost unheard of on a local level.

Then of course there was the major producer for the entire public television system, WGBH. And while their emphasis was on national production, they, too, had a fine local programming operation. Boston was the sixth largest market in the country, and Hartford-New Haven was roughly the twenty-fifth at the time and has steadily fallen since in relation to growing communities in the south and the west. If this were a prize fight, we would have been "Rocky," and the whole thing might have been called off before it started.

It wasn't until 1989 that the work we were doing would be ready to go up against the big boys in Boston. In the *New York Times* dated May 14, 1989, it was reported by the Associated Press that "Connecticut Public Television came of age this month, winning five regional Emmy Awards. That is more awards in one night than the state network has garnered in twelve years." I was quoted saying, "It sends a signal that there is a lot of talent in this region, that doesn't have to come out of 'creative centers,' that Hartford can be a real center for talented producers." It was a common refrain I had to repeat often to claim our legitimacy in this ascendant phase.

The winners for CPTV were Rick Doyle, director of *Numb…Children of Alcoholics*, a drama that he wrote and directed and Ron Gould produced about the impacts of alcohol on a family. Bruce Zimmerman's score won for best musical composition. It is still hard to recall how we had the temerity to mount a local drama of that type on a such a difficult subject, but it paid off. The regional Emmy was followed by the best local drama award by the American Film Institute.

I had green-lighted a longtime engineer, Peter Morrissey, on his vision to document his passion for sailboats in the program *Cannonball Wins the Newport to Bermuda Yacht Race*, a winner in the sports category. That willingness to allow technical people to actualize their dreams went a long way toward winning friends among a group central to your mission yet often most skeptical as to whether you can pull it off. Mike Dunphy, a fine cameraman, followed with *Cape Cod Reflections* a few years later.

Bob Englehart, the remarkably talented editorial cartoonist for the *Hartford Courant*, was enlisted to liven up our weekly public affairs program, *Connecticut Newsweek*, and he won for a mash-up of his commentaries. They were insightful and hilarious. And my dear friend Andrew Jones's *Thumbs Across America* was our final award winner for informational special. Oh, what a night.

Fortunately, it was the first of many great nights in Boston where we punched beyond our weight. In my tenure, we won over fifty regional Emmy Awards until I directed my undivided attention to national production in the late 1990s. Interestingly it was one local and the other national series that would solidify my reputation as a rainmaker. Neither looked in any way like the work we were honored for by colleagues in Boston in 1989.

The eclectic possibilities within public television remain one of its most endearing qualities. And while WWYZ was the first phenomenon with which I was associated, on the margins, watching and studying how it was tended and cared for, the opportunity to steward my own awaited.

Chapter 16: Facing a Difficult Reality

My time at CPTV was marked by long days filled with dealmaking, production review, and issues related to day-to-day operations. It was truly a juggling act.

Supervising creative people is unlike many other managerial pursuits. You cannot be guided by concerns about the clock or maximum efficiency within time constraints for long-form television, which is what we were about. Given that many of our projects involved archival material, we had to wait until that source content could be gleaned from an archive or a person's own collection.

And while running the department was time-consuming, the "other job" I had as chief spokesperson and salesman for our product on air, given the constancy of our fundraising appeals, made for long days crossing over into long nights.

Looking back at this advanced stage of decrepitude, age sixty-nine, I marvel that the younger me could put on a public show after the intensity of the daytime duties. After all, no one saw you at the desk by day, willing to grade you on a curve for your nighttime performance. In fact, to this day, many people still think of me as an on-air fundraiser only throughout my career. They imagine that I worked from seven o'clock to eleven o'clock and slept in until the afternoon to get ready for the next night's on-air appeals. And they assume I only worked three days a week, generally how I was scheduled, for a concentrated time frame in December, March, and August only. What a gig, were it true.

Even at that, creating an environment for support of a product that ostensibly was available to you at no cost required a high level of showmanship and psychological excavation to figure out what messages might work for various audiences. One moment you were pledging, as we called it, a great *Masterpiece Theatre* drama, and the next minute it was Bob Vila and *This Old House*. Each audience was totally different, and the way you spoke to each required a great sensitivity to those differences.

In my era, virtually all pledging was extemporaneous and free form. In the earliest stage after taking off the training wheels of pledging only children's programs, I can remember a wonderful man and relaxed pledge producer who would block out each ten- to fifteen-minute segment simply by encouraging the two talents to go back and forth, with little other guidance. Furthermore, if the previous break went well, he would say, "Whatever you did, do it again."

Imagine being on statewide television, with a sophisticated audience, and having both the freedom and responsibility to say something compelling enough to get that viewer to pick up a phone and support you. I loved the challenge as your impact was measurable and so important to the station.

As time went on, my presence was more ubiquitous on air. The better you performed, the more the development people wanted you on. I rarely said no unless it really interfered with life and a growing family. In retrospect, my wife, Carmelita, took on so much responsibility for things I could not do in this period. And all this as she built her own career as a gifted physical therapist, acquiring more credentials all the time and becoming an adjunct professor at Quinnipiac University.

In 1988 everything was going along well behind the camera and in front of it, when one day I noticed something quite disturbing looking back at me in my mirror. My face, never a thing of beauty but presentable, had lost volume on the right side, seemingly overnight. What the…? It is tough enough for anyone to accept a deformity on your defining characteristic to the world, your face, let alone a person who spends his life on camera.

My wife recalls being in the studio one night when a viewer asked to speak with me off the air. That is a risky thing to do anytime. I agreed to the exchange, nonetheless. She remembers me later telling her about the hurtful things the woman said about my appearance. She also remembers how sullen and expressionless I became. It was hurtful. I was at a loss to understand what happened to the symmetrical contour I had so much of my life.

As you can imagine, I began to seek answers. Again, my wife played a key role in tracking down the issue I was facing. A former neighbor, a plastic surgeon, was my first stop in what would turn into an over thirty-year odyssey. He confirmed my wife's research that it was Parry-Romberg syndrome, also known as Romberg's disease or progressive hemifacial atrophy. It is a rare atrophic disorder characterized by a progressive deterioration of the skin and soft tissue on one side of the face.

Interestingly current evidence points to the condition generally affecting the left side of the face and being more common in women than men. I lost that lottery on both counts—male, right side, etiology unknown. While mine stopped after the first wave, it settled in a place that really affected my self-confidence.

I searched high and low to find help, starting with a chin implant locally to give some volume back and then silicone injections regularly in Boston until the FDA ruled them unsafe. By 1995, I was still determined to find a better cure. That brought me to the door of Dr. John Siebert, practicing plastic surgery under the auspices of New York University Hospital. I say that because a Google search today will provide a complicated story of who Dr. Siebert is, how he interacted with his patients, and the validity of the credentials he asserted during his time in New York.

Suffice to say that my experience with what was called free flap surgery and the reconstruction of that side of my face was unsatisfactory. Aside from complications with the procedure, which caused me to endure two lengthy surgeries, the results were never ones he would include in his photobook of successes to share with prospective patients.

My wife, once again proving her amazing qualities, not only suffered all the confusion of the moment alone in New York City but also later attempted to bring down my still disfigured face with lymph drainage techniques. My visage was frightening. She never quit on me.

Finally, after countless smaller procedures by Dr. Siebert and another dermatologist in New York who could still use silicone, I accepted what was then possible, knowing full well that what I presented to the world was not something I was pleased with.

As I write this in 2021, it is only now that I can share the true progress I had hoped for then when I had the complicated surgery twenty-five years prior.

One day while at a local gas station, I saw on the newsstand a banner on the *New York Post*'s front page about a doctor, now at NYU, who had performed the most successful facial transplant in history while at another medical institution. In 2020, as medicine was struggling with a once-in-a one hundred-year event affecting the globe, Dr. Eduardo Rodriguez led the 140-person team of doctors at NYU in performing the first facial and double-hand transplant.

Feeling like the institution owed me a make good, and assuming progress had been made in the intervening twenty-five years, I went to see the remarkable Dr. Eduardo Rodriguez. He informed me that while it might take a few procedures, fat grafting, the process of taking fat from your abdomen and flanks and injecting it into your face, would be the preferred approach to giving me back the volume lost so long ago.

The first procedure was in May 2019, and the second, in the midst of the pandemic, was in July 2020. I can finally report that this long ordeal has come to a successful conclusion unless a significant amount of the fat is reabsorbed, thus requiring still another procedure.

All I wanted was my face back, not Tom Cruise's or Brad Pitt's—just my own. While he had a special on the Tom Cruise look, it was too expensive, I say jokingly. I told Dr. Rodriguez that going to him for this small procedure was like going to a man who could build a Maserati from scratch for an oil change. That "oil change" ironically has come just as I tucked myself away from the horrors of the virus and put a mask on the newly rebuilt face. I could help Alanis Morissette compose another verse for her song "Ironic."

It has had a psychological impact on me at times. I would avoid situations, acutely self-conscious about my appearance. Yet I put on makeup and went back on the air. Despite it all, my most robust time in front of and behind the camera still awaited me.

Chapter 17: ZZ Top Opened for Us

I mentioned earlier that music has played a key role in my life and career. As a hobbyist in this land of dreams, I have imagined the exhilaration an artist gets performing in front of an adoring throng of followers. Given the power and excitement music generates, I doubt there is anything that can stir emotions more.

While most of the professional performances I have been associated with were as a DJ playing the music and as a producer bringing others' music to the small screen, my flirtation with the performance end has given me the most joy.

There are so many people who put down their instruments in college and never resume in the cramped living quarters just out of school. Then despite having a few bucks in your pocket and a larger space in which to play, families and careers often intervened. Música interruptus is, I fear, far too common.

For some reason, I dragged my drum kits along from house to house, and my wife encouraged me to play, no matter the incoherence of hearing a drummer playing to music only he can hear.

Larry at the drums

It wasn't really until I turned fifty when I assembled a band to play at a party designed to commemorate the milestone that my late-stage musical journey began. The invite to the party read, "Larry can't bear to turn 50, so he's decided to play through it." At a downtown cantina in Waterbury, we rocked, and I had the joy of inviting my daughter, Leora, to front some tunes.

That ensemble, with a few changes, became BOOM—Band of Old Men— and in various incarnations we played out for the next eighteen years in our region in Connecticut. We played all kinds of venues. The only thing that these bars, restaurants, and outdoor settings had in common was the fact that none were really set up for music. Sound was always the issue. So while in our fifties and sixties, as we dreaded leaving the stage because of the work that remained for our weary bodies, and none more than the drummer, I would invoke my go-to line, "Are you sure this is the way the Beatles started?" In many ways, it was. However, they reached the heights of stardom before thirty, and we were still shlepping as we grew long in the tooth.

My interest in "doing what they do" was realized for one brief shining moment when a producer from Tennessee came to the station seeking to get a public television station to partner with him on a project of documenting known and unknown bands as they prepared and performed at the popular Riverbend Festival in Chattanooga in 2006.

I told him we might be interested as the concept was intriguing, and the headliners were good—Randy Bachman and ZZ Top, among others. My caveat was for BOOM to be considered one of the unknown bands invited to play at the festival. He agreed, vocals unheard, and off we went on the musical adventure of a lifetime.

We were recorded rehearsing in preparation and then had to really perform on the B-stage in front of what started out as a crowd of one hundred thousand people. Let me explain. The organizers shoehorned us in at eleven o'clock on a Thursday night following ZZ Top. Yes, ZZ Top opened for us. The first song out of the gate was "No Good to Cry," a regional hit by the great songwriter Al Anderson and his first band, from Connecticut, The Wildweeds. I later learned that ZZ Top had covered that song in the past. I kept thinking they must have said, "Hey, we did that song years ago. Why are these guys butchering it?"

The minute the stage manager said, "You're on," this otherworldly experience of playing on a real stage, with real sound guys and technicians, began. It went by in a blur for better or for worse.

The one hundred thousand people and the large screen projection gave way to an assembly of my wife, the only one of the band wives to make the trip, and a few hangers on. And as we walked back to our hotel, we were serenaded by the strains of the addled voice of an inebriated fan bellowing

The second incarnation of BOOM featuring left to right George Meyers, Tony Biello, Larry, Haig Papasian and Vern Coles

out, "Hey, man, you were great!"

And that was it. It was back to the speakeasies and the shoehorned setups at ill-fitting restaurants for the old boys in the band.

There was one more great experience. We started out as a six-man band and then parted company with two members over, well, differences. We later added the most talented vocalist and musician we had worked with at a stage when his capacities were being ravaged by a disease that would finally take his life.

When Tony Biello passed away, we—Vern Coles, George Meyers, Haig Papasian, and I—had a big decision to make. Do we add another member, or do the sidemen try to work on our voices and repertoire such that we could go out again in a stripped-down version? We chose the latter and worked out a new act with rock songs that were more approachable vocally.

By chance, a friend of mine told me about a Vietnam Veterans fiftieth event at the Bradley Airport complex outside Hartford in 2015, where it was expected that ten thousand veterans and families would come through. He knew I was in a band and indicated they were looking for rockers who played music from that era, and I told him we fit the bill. What he didn't know was that this four-piece version of BOOM had never played out before, and I never shared.

The organizers let us play, but what they did not tell us was that the band that would set up next to us and "open" for us was the US Coast Guard Band, one of America's great service ensembles. Hey, ZZ Top, the US Coast Guard Band, we take on all comers. We acquitted ourselves well that day, and it led to a joyous, and no drama, version of the band, playing out regularly over the next five years until COVID-19 shut us down after performing on March 7, 2020.

I feel so blessed that I never gave up on music, even if I could never perform to the level of those I emulate. It is truly a gift to oneself. I have a postscript to this chapter on music as we go along.

But first let the music play on as I take you back to my first experience and my tangential role in one of CPTV's biggest musical projects, *Tennessee Ernie Ford's America*, back in 1986. It took me from Connecticut to Tennessee again. And my encounters with my musical idols grew more frequent and interesting from there.

Chapter 18: How an Idea Becomes a Program

I was still leading the public relations office for CPTV when the *Tennessee Ernie Ford's America* project transpired. While a gentleman by the name of Chuck Allen, who worked for the Phoenix PBS affiliate, was overseeing the project, he did this project on his own and asked Sharon Blair, our national programming executive, to partner with him.

These kinds of alliances and partnerships are not totally uncommon in public television. It generally means a host of lawyers get involved in the dealmaking, and you must save the last fifteen minutes of the program for credits.

This is hyperbole on my part, but the credits on television are worthy of mentioning. The self-congratulatory nature of the business is unequaled. You might find it hard to believe how much time and effort goes into making that compilation accurate lest someone is offended. And when there is a partnership involved, how and in what order each party is identified is carefully negotiated and takes up far too much energy for something that the streaming services have figured out no one chooses to watch.

I was assigned to do the promotion for the Tennessee project. It was exciting to go down to Nashville and record the program in one of its storied theaters, the Ryman Auditorium. I coordinated the photography and all the collateral materials that would go out to PBS stations across the country to promote the show.

The stars involved included Lee Greenwood, the Gatlin Brothers, Marilyn McCoo, and Shirley Jones, among others. Given my interest in music and desire to be involved with high-visibility projects, I was taken by the professionalism of the effort. Carmelita came with me, and we had a great time watching the whole thing come together. Some artists were much more approachable and press hungry while others wanted to do their part and move on.

I watched the careful choreography of this production as the live audience experience blended with the divergent needs of television. I arranged for Nashville's local press to cover the event while at the same time recognizing that this capture of the experience was meant for audiences across the country in a few months' time. It was eye-opening and intoxicating.

While the music was more traditional than my taste, I appreciated the talent involved and felt that we were appealing to a good swath of the American public. It helped me recognize that the rich blend of public television programming could be a window on a diverse range of exhilarating experiences. And while on this occasion I was developing press materials for other stations, I was blessed to later take on a central role in creating many of those moments with performers who were my favorites. It also scratched my more commercial side.

I represent an interesting dichotomy as a broadcaster. I love the more glittery, commercial side of the house, if you will, but editorially adhere to and admire the fastidious traditions of the CBS News, Murrow and Cronkite style, and public television.

The main avenue for expressing those more commercial inclinations generally is with what is called pledge programming. The critique of which has always been- why does PBS only broadcast Sinatra, the Beatles, and

Pavarotti when we are asking for money? It has been a perennial conundrum for public television to "pledge" our core programs as opposed to specials, which may not appear weekly on our schedule. Clearly the system finds ways to do both by cherry-picking the most compelling and emotive of our regular content while also building pledge specials expressly to tug at your heart and purse strings.

The future successes that I am most associated with had that ongoing regular presence and elicited strong ratings and pledge impact. That is what made them so distinct as programming icons.

If public television is seen as a collection of creatives who want to do good and be distinct, the pathway to doing so is broad. You could design how-to programs to help people build, bake, and paint; children's programs to inspire a love of learning; or breathtaking nature documentaries. You could, like Ken Burns, take great care and time in making history projects that educate the whole country as to its history.

Pledge programming had a clear objective: entertain and inspire donations. Often that puts public television in the role of preservationists who take things that might have appealed to an earlier generation and repackage it to evoke nostalgia for a bygone era. Who could not appreciate the value of seeing Judy Garland in classic roles or a recreation of *Oklahoma!* or a timeless appeal of The Three Tenors or a documentary on the Carpenters, for that matter? These programs could justifiably be described as "pledge material" if the production were built to elicit much emotion and pledge dollars. And why expect to see it weekly since it is so "special"?

Often pledge programming was the tail that wagged the dog. If a Lawrence Welk special was warmly received, why not bring back the series and run it weekly and build a constant stream of support from a generation whose tastes were long since abandoned by commercial media in favor of pursuing younger demographics?

Public television has built new franchises that entire networks are now built on, such as HGTV and the Food Network, and at other times we have followed from behind to find audiences disenfranchised or underserved as their programming tastes were considered outmoded.

It was a real gift to be able to design pledge programs that would generate necessary dollars. And no one was better at it than Jim Scalem, a former programmer for PBS station KQED in San Francisco, who later became the vice president of pledge programming for PBS. He was also the impresario who green-lighted many of our pledge programs at CPTV. We became good friends with a shared passion for the San Francisco Giants. He was a Giants fan because of his many years in the Bay Area, and my allegiance stemmed from my father hailing from New York City. Dad was a big fan of the Giants, even as Horace Stoneham ushered them out of the Polo Grounds in the dead of the night, following the lead of Dodgers ownership in one of the most treacherous, stealth undertakings in New York history.

Aside from our love of baseball, since Jim hailed from New York, we had many of the same signature Big Apple broadcasters as role models. He loved radio as I did and was so influenced by the silkiness of WNEW personalities and the saltiness of those on WABC in New York. Jim had that same quirkiness that I had. While being raised on commercial broadcasting, we both recognized the special place public television had in expanding the strike zone with "commercially unviable" material that could attract appreciative and generous niche audiences. We enjoyed our place in society's seams stitching together a beautiful tapestry of programs that met our own sensibilities.

I was beginning to see myself as a public television immigrant in the early 1990s who could now look at the land I was inhabiting and know that I could play a role in designing material for the nation. Yet many stations had gone bust trying to play the game of national programming. Just the development work alone could take years and cost hundreds of thousands of dollars putting together glossy marketing materials, compelling sell videos, and hiring the talent who could put you in front of corporate decision-makers.

The sad truth about my beloved public television is that we are, in some ways, more dependent upon corporate entities blessing the content that we want to produce than our commercial counterparts. How so, you ask? Virtually all corporate support for public television is directed toward programs and little toward the weighty architecture of a system built to satisfy members of Congress, which requires the maintenance of facilities strewn about America. While one could argue this broad sweep of stations from sea to shining sea never made sense, it clearly lost all practicality when satellite delivery of programming came about and died another death when our cable competitors, who took genres we built and developed whole channels from each strand, could more cost-effectively operate from one location.

The logic that prevailed was always that local programming designed exclusively for our communities justified overlapping and duplicative backroom operations everywhere. If stations did the kind of local programming that we attempted in Connecticut in this period, deemed by *Connecticut Magazine* our "Elvis years" (before he gained weight and performed only in Vegas), then so be it. Few stations did more than the perfunctory public affairs gruel, which few watched.

Given that most public dollars—from people, the Corporation for Public Broadcasting (CPB), and local state governments and educational institutions—went toward maintaining facilities throughout the country, it was left to the corporations to decide which national programs made it to air and which did not. And while "Viewers like you" is a great tagline, the heavy lifting, and therefore much control, was ceded to those corporate interests.

Regrettably so many great ideas never made it to your home because of the lack of corporate funding that this was a form of control without prejudice. They just said no, and we moved on, unable to mount the production. At the same time, PBS standards were such that you could accept money from a company *only* if their support would not suggest a relationship that was too close to the content that it could be interpreted by the public as a conflict.

Who other than, say, a drug company or a medical concern wants to fund a program about breakthroughs in medicine? And if they have been the purveyor of some of those breakthroughs, how do you address that fact in the program?

There are foundations and other nonprofits, but many times the most logical funding source is deemed inappropriate because of the perception of conflict. For that reason and others, many stations chose not to produce programming for the system. They were passive receivers of content and lived off the value that other stations and independent producers created for them.

Before I took responsibility for national programming at CPTV, and with the support of United Technologies, a Connecticut-based corporation, McKinsey & Company, the prestigious consulting firm, was commissioned to guide the station in determining its rightful place, if any, in the national programming arena. McKinsey's admonition was this: do not try to start large projects from scratch because the odds of striking big on such programs was slight and the risks great. However, given our location between the behemoth stations in Boston and New York, there was a great talent pool in the region and projects that might be too small for those stations could fall to us.

McKinsey also encouraged us to find programs that were in some stage of development when we came upon them, the risk having been borne by another source, and determine how we could add value as a presenting or coproducing station.

Our mission became one of doing smaller scale series like how-to programs. We did series such as *Cooking with Todd English*, *Birdwatch*, *Blitz on Cartooning*, and *America's Walking* with Mark Fenton. Also high on our list was the pledge programming genre.

Given that the system funds pledge programs, irrespective of appeal to corporate interests, a tight relationship with the decision-maker at PBS is crucial. And that was something I was building with Jim Scalem. There was no calculus in this. We just liked each other. The fact that we got along, had some good ideas, and could execute more inexpensively than some of the larger stations made for a good combination.

The first test case was *A Tribute to Harry Chapin*.

Chapter 19: A Tribute to Musical Idol Harry Chapin

In 1991, when a friend told me that he knew someone in possession of unfinished camera masters—raw footage, if you will—of a tribute to Harry Chapin recorded in 1987 at Carnegie Hall, I sensed a great opportunity for the station to help bring the project to PBS. Given what McKinsey & Company said about not mounting projects from scratch but rather bringing partially completed work to completion, it was a perfect fit.

Harry's tragic death in a car accident a decade earlier and the rabid nature of his fans made his work the perfect subject for an emotive pledge special. His appeal in the Northeast markets, such as New York and Boston, was particularly strong. I should know. I was a great fan of his story songs. And to see him live in concert was to experience a man in full who had an unmatched capacity to do and care about more things in his short span on this earth than most of us will in five lifetimes.

The sons of drum immortal, Jim Chapin, Harry and his brothers were brought up in a musical family and, in fact, performed together at times. However, Harry's personality, even more than his musicianship, made him a singular figure on stage. He made you care about him and what he cared about as well as his music.

Every year I would go see Harry on one of his many trips to Connecticut. He was a tireless troubadour who would just as willingly play a backyard barbecue, if asked, as a five-thousand-seat arena. He just could not say no.

Many in his entourage worried about his unrelenting travel schedule in planes that were none too sturdy. Yet it was a car trip from his home on Long Island to New York City on a Friday afternoon in July 1981 that was his undoing as he was hit by a transport vehicle. Harry was on his way to the city to talk to his handlers, who were concerned about his propensity for doing "one concert for himself and one for the other guy." His money woes were apparent to them, if not to Harry.

The tribute upon which the program would be based was a mix of old folkies, such as Pete Seeger, the Smothers Brothers, and Richie Havens, and rockers, such as Pat Benatar, Bruce Springsteen, Graham Nash, and The Hooters. Harry Belafonte hosted the performance.

To make it into a compelling pledge special, I knew we had to do a few things. First, we had to be selective in the artists we chose from the performance and in the order they appeared. Second, we had to get captivating testimonials from other performers to punctuate the production and accent Harry's generosity of spirit and unique contribution to the story song genre. For that, we turned to people like Judy Collins and Billy Joel. Finally, we needed some Harry Chapin performances in the production. That turned out to be a harder task than I imagined.

Just as Harry would play for an audience of two, if asked, he would also go on every local television program originating in someone's basement, such as the old Mike Myers and Dana Carvey *Wayne's World* skit on SNL. It proved quite hard to find quality takes of Harry performing, but I was determined to include his performance of his classic "Taxi" in the show. We also used him doing "Mail Order Annie," which was one of his gentlest and most romantic tracks. We also merged a clip of his performance of "Tangled Up Puppet" for his daughter, purchased from *The Tonight Show*, with a female performer from the live production.

Jim Scalem signed off on the project, and I commissioned Ken Simon, a very capable producer I had used on several productions, to produce it. It was so thrilling to be able to honor one of my musical heroes in this way. While it was painful still at the time not to be able to visit with Harry every year, I felt close to him again throughout this project.

Candidly I thought often what it would have been like doing the project if Harry were still alive. How would I have felt? There is no doubt he would have had his hands all over the project. I recall a person well acquainted with him recounting how Harry would be watching a football game, composing a new tune, playing with one of his children, and directing other family activities in the same moment.

Harry Chapin and his 'Taxi' photo credit: Ruth Bernal

Brother Steve Chapin, not the avuncular personality Harry was but a skilled musician, did offer his thoughts throughout the process. However, my interactions with Charlie Sanders, the attorney for Sandy Chapin, Harry's widow, who wrote the lyrics for "Cat's in the Cradle," were the most contentious.

As executive producer, you wear many hats. You often conceive of the project; negotiate the business arrangements; oversee all elements of the production to make certain they satisfy all parties, particularly PBS; and take overall responsibility for the quality and delivery of a worthwhile program on time and on budget. One summer, when I decided to do a series of smaller concerts in our studio, I was offered a different definition of the role by NRBQ keyboardist, Terry Adams. He approached me before the production began and asked me if I was the executive producer. After I nodded affirmatively, he said, "Great, can you go out and get us a case of beer?"

My role in negotiating with Charlie Sanders put me in the difficult position of threatening the whole project because I felt that the various demands he was making were out of line. It was the first time it happened to me in a musical production, but I assure you not the last. My longtime assistant, Lisa Di Donato Cambria, was in the outer office and heard me for the first time in our great partnership hang up on someone. It was instinctive and impulsive. It was not my style. Somehow, I knew I had to change the dynamic, or the project was going to whither on the vine.

It's a lesson for all of us that sometimes we must step out of character by showing another side of ourselves if another party in a transaction thinks they have the upper hand and won't take us seriously. It worked. We got our deal and pieced together the program, risk free, as the performances were already there.

Based on the PBS contribution to the production budget, the return on investment in the program was deemed a success, and this first effort gave us the credibility to do many more such programs going forward. More importantly I think we did justice to a man whose whole life was about concern for others. I felt privileged to keep his memory alive in this way. I believe that it was the most heartrending musical special we ever produced as we wove song, biography, and artist narrative into the work. Having watched it again recently, it still works and stands as a timeless memorial to a musical giant gone too soon.

It also led to a relationship with the Chapin Foundation and, in particular, board member Mike Grayeb, who in 2016 had me emcee a performance by the living generations of the Chapin family in honor of Harry at Fairfield University in Connecticut. I was also the cohost of a Facebook live event in 2017 featuring brother Tom Chapin, a Grammy Award winner and an all-around nice guy. My last interview on this first-of-a-kind event for the Chapin Foundation was with Harry Belafonte.

While I could thank Harry in this way for the great joy he gave me, his legacy was the start of a great musical journey for CPTV on PBS.

Chapter 20: How the Suits like the Show

The Chapin project was perfectly aligned with what McKinsey & Company had suggested for CPTV. We had all the pieces of the puzzle, and all we had to do was assemble, glue, and distribute. The risk quotient was low.

Any wrong move by me dabbling in the national production game could have been tremulous for the station. We had no reserves. As a community licensee, unlike other stations, we did not have the state or an educational institution on the ready to back us up.

In all the aggressive plays we would make going forward, that was always on my mind. I was ever mindful of our fragile financial state. Everyone at the station was too. We were reminded of it daily in ways big and small.

And yet my desire to play in the musical game was strong. It checked off so many boxes for me. I grew up with the soundtrack of the 1960s as the defining characteristic of my father's career, loved to play music, and clearly liked being involved with high-visibility projects.

How many of us work in careers and fields in which giving an elevator talk about what you do proves pointless? The other day I met a young man who works for Indeed. I had seen their ads on television but had no concept of what the organization was about other than a vague sense that they helped people get jobs. He tried to explain to my analogue brain what his digital world involved, and it went in one ear and out both. If you and I, during my time at the station, got into an elevator and you asked me what I did and I said, "I program a television station, and I'm now producing a concert tribute to Harry Chapin," *that* you would remember.

I attended many marketplace screenings of different types of programs. We would consider a diverse range of programs. While a nature documentary on aardvarks mating could be fascinating given the patience of the filmmakers and the exquisite camera work, I wanted to attach to projects that had more mainstream appeal. Here, again, that commercial itch needed to be scratched.

The pledge genre made it possible.

Given our emerging relationship with PBS fundraising guru, Jim Scalem, I wanted to be careful in the selection of subjects for future musical projects. After all, the thrill and the agony of national pledge programming is that you know rather quickly, with just a few markets reporting, whether you have a winner or loser. And stations pay close attention to the pledge results being reported by other stations. You can have coverage from 99 percent of the country at the start of a drive, and a few reports that this program does not pledge well will result in the program vanishing from schedules in a heartbeat.

Jim would come to us to get involved in projects as a presenting station, wherein you act as the in-system patron to bring a project through the PBS labyrinth while leaving the actual production to a third party. In a sense, you act as an in-house administrator and marketer. He would turn to us to help edit and package a program, such as the Eagles concert, which was being offered by WNET. Or he would have us design and produce a national pledge event to produce all the interstitial content to encourage donations.

Harriet Unger, a skilled producer with a fundraising focus, became masterful at designing both DIY-type pledge specials and pledge events that the system would use. In many cases I was the talent for those events.

All this fell so neatly in our no-risk, make-a-few-bucks, develop-a-national-reputation basket. Of course, I wanted more.

I looked for opportunities to produce the big bang musical specials, like the major market producers and, of course, T. J. Lubinsky of WQED in Pittsburgh. Give credit where credit is due; he defined this era for PBS in terms of nostalgic music specials, starting with the doo-wop era and then putting together a mosaic of musical romps down memory lane from Motown to the disco explosion. His shows were well crafted and meant to evoke memories of an era. He was prolific and quite successful. His shows, in the words of Dylan, were "right on target, so direct." They were built for an express purpose, and they worked.

I recently became aware of the work of the late Clayton Christensen of Harvard University and the guru of "disruptive innovation." I love his theory of the job a product is designed to do. A classic example is Kodak. In describing their inability to transition to filmless photography, we are reminded that they became so enamored with their engineering prowess and technical capabilities that they lost sight of what people who purchased their product really cared about—capturing memories. Full stop. Apple figured that out, and the rest is the downfall of a classic American company.

In the case of fundraising programming for PBS, there are no awards for style points. Does it pledge? Is it constructed for that purpose? It may be a fun show to watch, but if people don't open their wallets as the key measurement, it's a bomb.

We followed Lubinsky's lead with *The British Invasion Returns* and *Hey La! Hey La! The Girl Groups Are Back!*, both mounted as three-day productions at Foxwoods Casino in eastern Connecticut. They did all right as pledge vehicles, and they were fun to watch, but they weren't gangbusters. I clearly did not have Lubinsky's golden touch. He had his eye solely on that ball while I was a bit spread out overseeing local productions and other major national work as we approached the mid-nineties. It's a lesson that singularity of purpose and focus, when rigorously applied, pays off.

I must say, though, I really had fun, particularly on the British Invasion show. While we couldn't get the two leaders of the invasion, the Beatles or the Stones, to participate, having Peter Noone and the new Herman's Hermits, Gerry and the Pacemakers, and Eric Burdon and the New Animals as part of it was terrific.

I called upon Gary Grant, who was the manager for Rob Bartlett of *Imus in the Morning* fame, to be our talent procurer for the compilation shows. Gary was a New York agent who had great contacts and a winning way. He brought a sense of whimsy and joy to the work and took care of as much of the dealmaking as he could, coming to me to try to strategize or sign off.

His one curiosity was a briefcase that he carried with him everywhere as if he had the atomic bomb codes assigned to him. He never let it out of his sight. As a fast-talking New Yorker, he could amble into and out of delicate relationships with a certain ease and a wink of *Con*-fidence.

For example, Eric Burdon was threatening not to perform on the last night of the production because he felt there was a problem with air filtration at Foxwoods. His throat was impinged upon. Gary and I listened. Gary told us he'd be back and went off in pursuit of a solution. He came back a short time later and assured Eric that he had talked to the engineering department at Foxwoods, and a refiltration of the air was in process. Eric inhaled, as a demonstration of his seriousness about the situation, and declared that he could tell the difference. Given his winning way, Gary, who likely went to the men's room in his time away, convinced Eric that he parted the Red Sea on his behalf. Problem solved.

In working with musical artists, I learned that egos are enormous, and concerns are varied and unpredictable. While loving the work, I was always on pins and needles that anything could go wrong.

Often it starts in the negotiation phase, as with Charlie Sanders for the Harry Chapin program, or during the production, as in virtually all cases. And sometimes it's after all is done in the packaging of the program, the use of various parts of the repertoire, or the home video distribution deal. It's difficult to know exactly what will spark the flare-up. Assuredly, something will. How you de-escalate those situations is key.

On the British Invasion show, who knew that the once handsome Reg Presley, lead singer of the Troggs, had turned into a rather obese middle-aged man who could barely growl through "Wild Thing" once without oxygen, let alone the extra time we needed because of a technical snafu? Or that Freddie of Freddie and the Dreamers would have a heart attack on the flight back to England and threaten to sue us?

Peter Noone, who performed and hosted the show for us, was great to work with. Given his uninterrupted career fronting newbies still called Herman's Hermits, he never lost a beat in recognizing that it's "show business." He understood that you take your charming personality, some musical ability, and confectionary tunes and ride it to the end. He's never been without work and a recognition of his musical lane, and he knows how to traverse it from every angle on cruise ships, state fairs, compilation shows, and the like.

I applaud the "truth in music" laws being passed to protect consumers who are attracted to older bands and have no way of knowing if the members they see on stage have any lineage to the original groups. This has been spearheaded by Jon Bauman, the guy who played "Bowzer" with the rock and roll revival act Sha Na Na.

Many of the acts we had on various compilations were only legitimized and authenticated by the lead singer. It is so much harder if the surviving member, or the one still owning the name, is the bass player who never sang or, worse yet, someone who joined the band ten years into their run and somehow goes out using their name.

In 1993 I was on the prowl looking for a smash musical special from my era. In looking at stars who had not done a PBS pledge special, I considered whether the performer still had commercial appeal or if it had ebbed for a younger generation but still burned bright in the hearts and minds of baby boomers. Carole King was one such performer.

Jim Scalem was on board, but I underestimated the strength of Carole's personality and will in fashioning the program she wanted.

Recently a nationally syndicated article by Mikael Wood of the *Los Angeles Times* titled "'Tapestry' at 50: How Carole King 'bet on herself' to record a singer-songwriter classic" pointed to the issue that we faced. He wrote that "in the years after 'Tapestry,' King could seem ambivalent about the stardom she'd attained. She continued to make records, occasionally in search of a convincing style, but she didn't tour or promote them as the pop industry requires." Her aloof personality severed her ongoing relationship with her fans. James Taylor, her close friend and collaborator, maintained and grew his audience with constant touring and reinvention.

Of course nothing appealed to her audience more than her smash album of 1971, *Tapestry*. Wood also reminded that "nine of her 10 most-streamed songs on Spotify are from 'Tapestry.'"

While she agreed to do the pledge special with us in our home base at the Bushnell Theater in Hartford, she had just released a new album and wanted that to be the focus of the program. Furthermore, she wanted her own director, Larry Jordan.

Editorial control, an oft-used term in our industry, is something that PBS always demanded that the producer retain, though music specials were not considered controversial, so sharing that with an artist was not uncommon.

In doing so with Carole, it was with some foreboding given her desire to demonstrate her ongoing relevance as an artist and not a beautiful fading memory. She demonstrated that by wanting to keep *Tapestry* out of the title of the show. I won that battle by having her agree to *Carole King: A New Colour in the Tapestry*. She wanted to have contemporary rock sidemen on the show, such as Slash and Teddy Andreadis of Guns N' Roses. That was fun until Slash showed up at a rehearsal with a "F***PBS" T-shirt.

I then turned to Ira Koslow, her agent, who worked for Peter Asher, to intervene on the wardrobe selection for the actual performance. He assured me Slash would not wear that T-shirt on performance night. I really enjoyed working with Ira. He was a true professional and a genuinely nice guy, who himself had difficulty at times guiding Carole in ways that might benefit the success of the program, given its fundraising purpose.

Carole King on stage at The Bushnell, Hartford, CT
photo credit: Catherine Wessel

We all know the advice to walk a mile in the other person's shoes so that you understand what motivates them.

I truly wish that I had seen *Beautiful: The Carole King Musical*, the wonderful Broadway production, mounted more than a decade and a half later, about Carole's life. I would have come to a much quicker and better understanding of the woman I was many times up against.

She had to fight to be seen and recognized as the frontline talent, not a behind-the-scenes genius, that she is. She demonstrated that her instincts about her headlining appeal were right. Too often she was regarded highly for her songwriting capabilities but discounted because of her voice or appearance or whatever measure they used. Many thought she would not be a star in her own right.

What she had earned, she certainly was not going to relinquish to an unknown executive producer like me. Now I get that. It should have been clear to me that this was what the power dynamic of editorial control would look like when producer Ken Simon joined me in Los Angeles, ahead of the taping, to take in one of her concerts. In meeting with her after the show, she said, "So how did the suits like the show?" I guess I never thought of myself as a "suit," but she had long ago divided the playing field between those who have the power and the performers who deserve a much greater voice. Even having that advance understanding would not have made it any easier to get what I needed from her in this performance.

I needed a show that used every bit of *Tapestry* to populate all the sets, and each set needed to start in a rollicking way and become more emotional and end on the most heartrending note. This device was clearly tucked in my memory bank from my Natural 92 days. On set two, she stayed resolute that it would end with a rocker included on her new album. On set three, she agreed to end with "You've Got a Friend." Guess which set performed well and which did not. She wouldn't budge on that split decision, and that, in large part, determined that the show, while a wonderful concert production, was a moderate fundraising success.

I must admit that Larry Jordan was a good choice on her part as director, though I do think Jay Whitsett or Haig Papasian on our staff would have yielded virtually the same result. Larry gave us one of those unpredictable moments when he lost communication to our cameramen and admonished me that he had done concerts in South America, in a war zone, that were easier than this one, or some such words. I may have made up the part about the war zone. It was all in a day's work.

Carole, the perfectionist that she was, took back all the original audio from the production and resang her parts.

If you are observant and watch this performance, now available on YouTube, you can see that we had to go behind her for a few seconds on the first song, "Hard Rock Cafe," because we could not sync voice and picture. It's a wonderful curiosity.

Let's fast-forward to 2016. By then I had left television and was back in radio full time. The station was offered complimentary tickets to a theatrical release of *Tapestry: Live in Hyde Park*. That's right, it was all from that one classic album.

Of course I went to see it. From a production standpoint, I don't think it holds a candle to what we did. In part that is because outdoor concerts lack the ability to use the great architecture of the building as a great set piece, such as we did. However, it was the program, musically, that I wanted to do some twenty-four years earlier. Unfortunately Carole wasn't ready at that time. As we know in life, timing is everything.

We went on to produce musical specials with the likes of Celia Cruz, the Cuban salsa queen, again at the Bushnell. Celia, at the time, was well up in years. The one moment from that production that I wish I could unsee was her manager, Ralph Mercado, coming back into the production truck just as the show began to tell me that she was off-key. I said, "Ralph, that's your artist. What do you want me to do?" I went on to say, "We'll fix it in post."

Subsequent concerts with Bobby Vinton and Gene Pitney were more drama free. I must admit that going to Bobby's Blue Velvet Theater in Branson to record the concert was quite a trip. Harriet Unger, our producer on this project, and Haig Papasian, our director, joined me for a once-in-a-lifetime experience because unless extradited to Branson for something I did while I was there, I assure you that was my only visit. The streets leading to the theaters were on a precipitous incline. People attracted to the location were so out of shape; anything that passed as entertainment would be applauded as they plopped down in their seats. And to reinforce that point, it was a place where Yakov Smirnoff was still considered funny. Enough said.

Working with Gene Pitney was a great thrill for me as he was Connecticut's own and still recorded out of a home studio in Vernon, a town outside Hartford. He was a gentleman and, to the untrained eye, seemed in great shape. He died in 2006, a few years after recording the concert.

In the 1960s he had big hits with songs such as "Town without Pity," "24 Hours from Tulsa," and "Last Exit to Brooklyn" and wrote hits such as "Rubber Ball" for Bobby Vee. His songs were dramatic and orchestral, giving some musical heft to the popular genre.

When we were kids, Steve Mednick, a childhood friend of mine and band member in The Avengers and early in BOOM, went with me to see Gene Pitney at The Bushnell in Hartford when a performer by the name of Turley Richards was one of the warm-up acts. While we all were waiting for Gene to come on stage, a chant went up and said, "Give him the hook." Looking back now, I regret my decision to join that chant, reflecting on how many times that same cry could have echoed throughout places where I played.

In my career we mounted musical productions in Toronto with the Scottish Fiddle Orchestra, a wonderful ensemble. We became involved in mash-ups, taking various roles in packaging and distributing projects featuring people such as James Taylor, Patti LaBelle, Johnny Mathis, and Ringo.

While we maintained a strong relationship with Jim Scalem at PBS, we had also developed a strong alliance with APT, a next-in-line distributor out of Boston. There were many reasons to distribute via PBS rather than APT. One had money, the other not so much. One made the process easier; the other made it more difficult. It was always a strategic determination as to who we would approach on one project or another.

We learned that APT had an interest in distributing a Ringo's All-Starr Band concert, but they needed a station partner to handle distribution and do a pledge event for the show. To my utter delight and amazement, Ringo was made available to record a lengthy interview for the pledge event, and I got to conduct the interview. Ringo was in Los Angeles, and I did my part from Hartford. He appeared on set and said, "Am I talking to Larry?" I could see him, but he couldn't see me. It was one of my most terrifying moments on camera. The last thing I wanted to do was to make a bad impression on someone whom I have admired for so long. The risks, given my psyche, were great.

To say that this was a thrill was an understatement given that the Beatles were clearly the cultural touchpoint for my generation, and Ringo, with his great personality and elevated perch on the bandstand, gave my musical instrument the place and dignity it was so long denied.

Haven't you heard all those drummer jokes? What do you call a drummer's girlfriend? "The breadwinner" and on and on.

While crafting this interview, I recognized how difficult an assignment it was, given how many times Ringo had been interviewed and asked every question under the sun about the Beatles. I decided that I would try to give it a bit of a twist, you know, one drummer to another, without skewing it such that it wouldn't appeal to a broad audience. I asked him how, as each of the songwriters in the band was going in different musical directions—one more influenced by Eastern music, one more avant-garde, and the like—he could adapt his drumming style to their changes. His answer was quintessentially Ringo. "Larry, we were a band. That's what we did."

I thought I had done my research well in coming up with the question "Ringo, I understand there was only one song that John wanted to get back for tempo, and that was 'Help!' Is that true?" Given that John had died years before, his response was terse as it was clear. "Oh, Larry, that was so long ago. You'll have to ask him." In layman's terms, I think was Ringo telling me to drop dead. I carried on.

In any event, years later I was googling something or other and came upon a video on John's favorite Beatles songs. I was mortified to hear, in his words, that "Help!" was among them because at the time, in 1965, it was his plaintive plea to get out of the prison they had built through their overwhelming success.

Was my question wrong and Ringo had every right to upbraid me? John then went on to say that the record company wanted it to be an up-tempo hit, and therefore they recorded it at too frenetic a pace.

Never would I criticize Ringo for rushing the rhythm. He was so perfect for the perfect band. I defended him many times to non-drummers who didn't realize his dramatic importance to the band. Just listen to the energy of the early Beatles. It's astonishing, owing to his chops.

By the way, rushing the tempo is something I've been accused of, and rightly so, many times. I take comfort in a recent biography of Levon Helm of the Band, where he reminds people that drummers are not metronomes. No, we have heartbeats and get excited by the music and do sometimes rush it a bit. Thanks, Levon. I wish you could convince my bandmates of this.

This Ringo experience led to another of my musical odysseys, which gave me such great joy. This one would happen years later in Las Vegas.

Chapter 21: This Could Be You

In many ways my career represented a fantasy. I could stay in my home state, be associated with quality work, have a growing presence as an on-air personality, and nationally produce programs that had impact beyond our borders. What more could I want?

With a wonderful young family, living in an unassuming suburb in Connecticut, I could get up every morning and be grateful that my thirty-minute trek to Hartford led me to a world of possibility so far beyond what others waking up around me would do that day.

And with it all, I still had other passions, such as my drumming and, dare I say, my New York Knicks, which always took up more mind space than they should.

While as a kid my most vivid sports memory was watching the 1962 World Series featuring my father's favorite team, the San Francisco Giants, lose in game seven to the New York Yankees, baseball became secondary to my growing love of basketball.

Just as I lost my dad, there was a consoling event taking place at Madison Square Garden as my favorite basketball team was becoming one of the greatest units ever assembled, with the likes of Walt Frazier, Willis Reed, Bill Bradley, Dave DeBusschere, and so many other colorful players.

To this day, when I need to quiet my mind over something that is daunting me, I will repeat an oft-heard Marv Albert call: "DeBusschere to Reed, over to Barnett, back to Frazier—YES!" It is something all Knicks fans yearn to hear and see again as we haven't won a title since the two banners were hung from the rafters at the Garden in the early 1970s. I imagine that I could have become so much more had I not spent so many unvalidated hours watching hapless team after hapless team, year in and year out.

Nonetheless the appeal is still there. My fandom has never waned. And it is an inheritance my son will probably rue long after I have left this mortal coil. I must say that going to a few games with him at the Garden each year has represented one of my great bonding experiences with him. The Knicks do have purpose as the nineteen thousand plus who always attend, despite their record, can attest.

My love of basketball also brought into my life my most cherished friend, Sid Frenkel, who knew we had something important in common when we first got together, through our children and preschool, because of the New York Knicks jacket I was wearing.

Right here, right now, for these two reasons, the Knicks owe me nothing.

Back in 1989, I saw an advertisement for a Knicks Fantasy Camp, being put on by then coach Rick Pitino. It was in Atlantic City. Given the coach's involvement, the suggestion was that many current Knicks would show up. However, between the time the camp was publicized and when it took place, Pitino, as has been his long history, took another job. Nevertheless, he maintained his commitment to run the camp. I signed up. Now people go to Atlantic City to gamble, and in a sense, that was my motivation for riding the rails there that July.

Can you believe that I practiced all summer thinking maybe I could perform well at this three-day event? I never played organized basketball on any level. And while I had a good shot, it only fell with regularity when I was unguarded and standing flat-footed. Despite my love of the game, I was more comfortable, though not proficient, on a baseball diamond, tennis court, or bowling alley. Basketball, like an elusive lover, always demanded more talent and height than I, at five feet, six inches, could put forth. I asked myself, how embarrassing can this be?

The camp was held at Caesars Atlantic City, and I had an inkling of how this would go when my roommate, Mike O'Rourke, from Stamford, Connecticut, introduced himself. He was a handsome guy who looked like he had just jumped out of an Irish Spring commercial. He also looked like a ballplayer.

An hour later it was time for the opening reception in the Marcus Aurelius room. Outside the room was a statue of the noble Roman himself. Anatomically correct in every way, even the damn statue made me feel inadequate.

Guys started arriving. One by one we sized up one another. I thought you had to be thirty or over to come to camp. I soon realized the only qualification was that you had $1,595 to put down for the chance to be humiliated. One kid was only nineteen.

I was struck by the names of the players. Well over half of us were Jewish. A study should be done on why Jewish men love basketball so much. I wonder if, on Mount Sinai, God gave Moses the Ten Commandments and, as a bonus, threw in Red Auerbach's videotape, *Winning Basketball with Larry Bird and Red Auerbach*.

Then Coach Pitino, diminutive but fiery, entered the room. His charge was simple but direct. "We are here to have fun," he reminded. "But whenever I step onto a court, I play to win." His no-nonsense approach was always apparent in watching him operate on the Knicks bench. It scared the hell out of a totally undisciplined and previously uncoached player like me.

Yet there was a glimmer of anticipation and promise. I had been running three miles a day and spent time on a court making bank shots against phantom defenders, dribbling behind my back, and crossing over hand-to-hand without the pressure of a fleet guard prepared to go the other way for a quick two. With my son's encouragement, I even made ten free throws in a row. Yet deep down I sensed my fortunes would change when tested under game conditions. I was right.

My first mistake was donning a Knicks sweatshirt and pants when attending breakfast on day one. I should have worn a tie and jacket and protested, as others did on opening night, that my wife surprised me by signing me up for camp, and I really wasn't prepared.

When I got to my locker, there it was—Rifkin number 8. At least no Knick immortal had worn the number. Imagine the ribbing if it were number 10; "Hey, that didn't look like a Walt Frazier move to me."

The Knicks trainer, Mike Saunders, a great character in the gentlest of senses, led us in a series of stretches. He called one stretch for NBA players the "blow your own horn" position while suggesting that this description was inappropriate for us.

Pitino's whistle pierced my heart. It was time for business. First came the drills. I suddenly realized that the ego I had read about in the New York papers, as he played out his decision whether to leave the Knicks for the University of Kentucky, was real. The man was here to impress. We were on his turf, on his terms. Nobody cared that in broadcasting, the career of my choosing, I had accomplishments of my own. The comfort I could take in that and in my everyday surroundings had been stripped away. On this day I would be judged only by what I did with a basketball in my hands.

He had assembled a great coaching staff, including Dick Barnett, who played alongside Walt Frazier on the Knicks 1970 championship team. I struck up a nice relationship with Dick, who went on to get his PhD in education.

In the first actual games of the camp, my play was a horror show. I couldn't get into rhythm on offense and was beaten a few times on defense. My team lost, and I was later traded for the purposes of "balance."

The combination of my horrid play, a gym with no air conditioning and temperatures in the eighties, and a lunch better left to the flies trying to compete for it, I recognized that my definition of the word "fantasy" differed markedly from that of Max Shapiro of SportsWorld, the promoter of the event.

Since my play improved slightly on day two, I took the bait and accepted Coach Pitino's one-on-one challenge. He dispatched me four baskets to zip. His only loss was to Bobby Wong, an exciting player, who led a team I was on to a double-overtime defeat of Coach Pitino's team later in the day.

Let me just say that while I added as much as I could through sheer effort on defense, I did not hit a shot in a five-on-five game the entire camp. On day three, in three-on-three play, I made my first game hoops of the camp.

I tried to hide my embarrassment because I don't think you're supposed to show disappointment during a fantasy.

My spirits were buoyed when the great Earl "the Pearl" Monroe dropped by and passed the ball to us in a drill. I thanked him for the thrills he'd given us Knicks fans and realized, watching him hobble into the gym, that I should've thanked him for sacrificing a comfortable retirement for our pleasure.

It reminded me of a documentary we purchased to broadcast about the travails of Jim Otto, number 00, the famed center for the Oakland Raiders football team. The routine he had to go through, in retirement, just to get out of bed each morning was beyond sad. And a podcast I would do in later years with Steve Almond, author of *Beyond Football*, and the brain injuries sustained by players, on top of the orthopedic ones, made me swear off my modest interest in football.

At the end of these camps, there was always a banquet and awards ceremony. Imagine that. After dinner, Coach Pitino said he enjoyed running it, his first adult camp. Each of us received the obligatory trophy and certificate. Then it was time for special commendations. There were

*Former Knick Eddie Lee Wilkins and Larry at
The Mecca, Madison Square Garden*

only six special awards. My roommate, Mike O'Rourke, won "Mr. Hustle." He deserved it. He was the only guy in camp who could prove that he had sweated right through his sneakers. When my name was called for best sportsmanship, I was pleased and surprised. Sure, it's the equivalent of Miss Congeniality at a beauty contest, but it's recognition, nonetheless. The fact that I showed so little was disappointing, and the award wasn't like hitting the jumper to win game seven of the NBA Finals, but as it pertains to my favorite sport, for this lifetime, it will have to suffice.

I look back and recognize that I missed a whole programming strand based on this concept in the form of reality television, which would become so big years later. It was the notion of taking us out of our comfort zone, stripping away the things that wall off our insecurities, and seeing how we perform on unfamiliar turf.

It was a long way from that Atlantic City experience to the next time, in 2013, that I would embark on one more fantasy—the Rock 'n' Roll Fantasy Camp at the MGM Grand in Las Vegas. It was run by Ringo's manager, David Fishof, with whom I had become acquainted years earlier while working on the All-Starr band project. He kept telling me that I should come to one, and I never really thought that another fantasy camp was in my future until he designed one primarily for drummers.

The great session drummer Hal Blaine came to the event to promote a documentary on the Wrecking Crew, and drummers Alan White (Yes), Denny Seiwell (Wings), and Joe Vitale (Crosby, Stills, Nash & Young) were among the drumming dignitaries. I was determined not to be psyched out as I was years back at the Knicks camp.

Given that they had more drummers signed up than guitarists and keyboardists, they assigned two drummers to each band formed at the camp. While I had done no research on the fellow drummer I would be sharing the back line with, it was David Bronson, who had played with the Righteous Brothers for twenty-five years. "What was a ringer like him doing here?" I asked. He said he lived in Southern California and knew the camp counselors and performers, such as Blaine; J. R. Robinson, then the most recorded drummer in history; and the immortal Jim Keltner.

We had two days to prepare to perform on stage in the lounge area of the MGM Grand on the last night. Our band would perform "Gimme Three Steps" by Lynyrd Skynyrd and "Breakdown" by Tom Petty. We also did a vamp at the end on "Good Times Bad Times" by Led Zeppelin. I acquitted myself much better at this camp than the one outlined earlier in this chapter, but David's years on the road were a clear reminder of what greatness takes in any field.

At the basketball camp, I was reminded that while I always appreciated the physical conditioning required to keep up with the inhuman pace and schedule of the pro game, I underestimated the mental toughness needed to endure.

Every twenty-four seconds in the NBA, the ball changes hands. In a forty-eight-minute contest, each team will have at the minimum, sixty opportunities to properly execute its offensive plays. And during each game, your coach will huddle with you ten or more times, as well as halftime, to strategize. It is not easy having a performance review ten times a day. Suddenly it became clear why so many great physical specimens washed out of the NBA. They could not take the thinking, reacting, and adjusting needed to play consistently at that level.

In music it is much the same as players from totally different backgrounds are thrown into ensembles throughout their career and required to call upon their endless hours of training and facility, playing all kinds of music in all kinds of settings, to feel at one with their instrument.

David had that feel and touch that corresponded with a life in music. To the untrained eye, I was fine on the bandstand playing alongside him. As one who has studied the greats in our field, I knew the ground I would have to make up to approach his facility.

A couple pointed to me during the performance with great encouragement. I assumed they were from Connecticut and knew me from television. They were from the Midwest, they later told me, and had no idea who I was but liked my energy on stage. I was grateful for their appreciation, wishing I had more to offer.

Our band was the first out of the gate under the tutelage of Jason Ebs, who played with Peter Criss of Kiss. We performed creditably. Owing to the "there's always a faster gun theory," a few performances later came a group of guys under the tutelage of Jeff Foskett, whom I credit with making possible my musical idol Brian Wilson's successful return to the performance stage in the 2000s. He provided gentle guardianship of Brian on tour. Evidently, they were a working band back home and performed the second side of the Beatles's *Abbey Road*. At best, we immediately became a runner-up.

Both experiences reminded me that whatever the field, there are no shortcuts, and it's not all glory. You must put in the work. And the easier it looks, the more work has been left unseen in the exhausting process of practicing with intent.

Chapter 22: Ipi N'tombi

A December 28, 1976, article in the *New York Times* had the headline, "Black Committee Urges Boycott of 'Ipi Tombi,'" as it started its previews at the Harkness Theatre, located at Broadway and Sixty-Third Street, in New York City.

Who knew that I would later be involved in the production that had been objected to by Americans based on the theft of black cultural heritage, exploitation of blacks by South Africans, and America's cooperation and support of the then apartheid government of South Africa?

Much of the controversy surrounding this musical, said to be the South African equivalent of America's *Porgy and Bess*, was based on its creator, Bertha Egnos, a white South African. Critics suggested that she brought together various dance groups to perform their native dances and songs and later claimed and copyrighted them under her name. The protest claimed that she appropriated the work and had no claim to it. It belonged to the black people of South Africa. When black people at the time had no say in their country, it was believed to have been a major injustice. The title *Ipi Tombi* is a Zulu phrase, literally spelled "Iphi Ntombi," and it means "where is the girl?"

Now I am not here to divine who was right or wrong in their claims but simply to tell you that much had changed in the late 1990s when we were made aware of the production being mounted again in South Africa and our ability to become an American partner in the production.

Given the overturning of apartheid, Nelson Mandela's release from prison, and his ascendance to the presidency, *Ipi N'tombi* was now seen as a cultural treasure and had shed its ugly reception in the United States back in the 1970s.

I was introduced to the project by Andrew P. Jones, who had moved to South Africa and was helping disabled young people learn to become filmmakers. He told me of the excitement building around this new production and that it was going to be videotaped at the University of Capetown, and PBS could be a part of it and fashion it as a fundraising program if we brought some money to the table and got involved early on.

I convinced Jim Scalem to back the production, and I was dispatched to South Africa to oversee the television program to ensure that it would meet the expectations of American audiences. This was not my first international sojourn, but it was, I assure you, the most pleasurable.

In the late 1980s, I responded to an invitation to join a press tour of Israel by an American-based goodwill group out of New York City. However, I made it clear to the organizer in New York that to justify the time away from my growing responsibilities at the station, I would need to break away from the tour to develop a documentary to be called *Connecticut's Israeli Connection*. I would look at a sister city connection between Beersheba and a town in our state and focus a good portion of the documentary on people from Connecticut who had made "aliyah" from Connecticut to Israel. "Making aliyah" by moving to the land of Israel is a fundamental tenet of Zionism and had much currency for many of us during the Trump years.

I felt it would be a good growth experience for me to produce something of my own since I was overseeing a bevy of producers.

I ran into a host of roadblocks shortly after touching down in Tel Aviv. The sabra, an Israeli-born woman, now running the tour in Israel, had not been informed of my need to break away from the tour from the stateside organizers. She objected to the dates I planned to be away and forced me to rearrange my crews and all logistics with the people I had lined up to be interviewed. It was a mess.

Larry with performer from Ipi N'Tombi in South Africa

There I was, making calls on Israeli pay phones, trying to reschedule a host of interviews, and imagining that my whole purpose for making the trip was in jeopardy. After hours of distraction, I was able to reconstruct the tapings but not without realizing the inglorious hours spent by producers, not always fortunate enough to have production assistants because of public television budgets, on the blocking and tackling of television.

Every time I watch a cable news channel and see guest after guest from around the country, I cannot help but think of the endless round of back and forth to coordinate the guest and the live satellite connection to make this happen. We watch television with such casual disregard for how many people it takes to coalesce around a successful production. And while I bemoan the self-congratulatory nature of the industry, I do appreciate the expertise and the texture required to mount one dramatic period scene, which may last ninety seconds, and the care that goes into the sets, not to mention the lighting and wardrobe. Try taking all that into account when you are about to switch channels and think about the indignity that it represents to skilled artisans and others who worked tirelessly on getting right what you just dismissed with the remote on your couch. Regardless you're likely to do it anyway.

So finally, my documentary did come together but not without incident. We had Palestinians as production assistants on the shoot. They were great to work with. However, we left some tapes behind at a site. The crew chief I had hired told me not to fret. In his words, "They might kill you, but they won't do something petty like stealing your tapes." What was I to make of such statement? They kept the tapes in safekeeping for us. And I dismissed his more dire pronouncement as a predisposition built out of long simmering enmity foreign to an American Jew's experience or understanding.

By comparison, my experience a decade later in South Africa was tranquil and exhilarating. Even back in the 1970s, despite the controversy, *Ipi N'tombi* played for six years around the world to standing ovations. It was a joyous and rousing production.

Here I was as the "American television executive" in South Africa to capture the new version some twenty years later for the express purpose of making it a successful fundraising production. I was treated kindly by the staff and crew. I discovered that the company of fifty included many direct descendants of the original cast members.

It is the story of a Johannesburg mine worker who sings of his love for the girl back home and his sense of separation from his tribal roots.

While the new production was true to its roots, it was restyled to include some new songs, such as "Four Important Porters from Potgietersrus," which will stop you in your tracks.

One write-up said that *Ipi N'tombi* might well be regarded as the national opera of South Africa. The costumes, the dance, and the storyline, personifying the essential African conflict between the rural and urban worlds, are timeless. And the wonderful wedding ceremony between the boy and his girl symbolizes a marriage of tribal and city cultures.

If you doubt the energy I describe, go to YouTube and watch for yourself. I am so proud that it lives there.

Another joy was spending time with Andrew as I hired him to capture a behind-the-scenes look at the production as a bonus for stations.

Still the question remained, would it translate for American audiences? Do you remember when I indicated that early precinct returns could give you a gauge on whether a pledge special was going to work? It was always nerve-racking to wait for the first reports. I recall being at the station on a Sunday and reading one of the first reports on *Ipi* from Rochester, New York, and lo and behold, it was given a thumbs-up for the pledge results there. I extrapolated from that first sounding that we had a hit on our hands. We imagined great support in major markets, which it ultimately had, but were less certain in smaller markets.

I got to travel to a few markets, including Atlanta and Boston, to stand before their audiences and "pledge" the program. All in, this was a magical production. To this day, reading reviews of the show on Amazon gives me a chill.

John Graham saw the first stage show at New York City's Harkness Theatre, before it was shut down. In 2002 he wrote, "Since then, I have never been able to get its music out of my mind." He later bought the soundtrack but said, "I happened to catch a glimpse of a familiar scene as I surfed past PBS—and clicked right back to find myself in the middle of a riotous river of swirling color and African harmonies (unmistakable, and unlike any other!) and saxophones and drums and ankle bracelets and movement (you better BELIEVE we got rhythm!) and almost the SMELL of Africa....It pins you back to the couch, this show does, and never lets you go."

Sandra Chiesa wrote in 2015, "I watch for the wonderful music; one never tires of it. If you're having a bad day and need cheering up—this is the ticket."

And Willie Smith said in 2012, "*Ipi N'tombi* is uplifting and leaves one feeling so very, very good…every time it's viewed. Buy it! Watch it! You'll never regret it."

It felt so great to be associated with something that touched hearts in this way. A big tip of the hat to Jay Whitsett, who, upon my return, took charge of the editing process for the final program. His contributions to so many of our successes were profound.

My passion for this project was infectious. Jay caught it and brought it home.

Chapter 23: Better Yet

The editorial standards established by PBS are stringent, yet they get cast aside during the months of fundraising programming.

What never could stand the scrutiny of meticulous gatekeepers of content at PBS is brushed aside as an irritant if it stands in the way of raising dollars to support the other parts of the schedule that scream "mission."

We at CPTV were complicit in producing some of the self-help genre of programming that escaped serious review. I will not name the programs because it would be unfair to the presenters, who themselves never imagined that what they were putting forward was anything but beneficial content. It is just that it did not get cross-examined in the way that other programs do.

The only program that I look back on with concern about its impact was one with a prestigious New York doctor on pain management. If you recall, in the 1990s, pain control seemed like the last frontier for medicine. It was all the rage. And it remains an enviable goal. The tragedy has been the complicity of doctors in the excessive prescribing of opioids. Clearly our program was not at the center of this American tragedy, but I should have asked more questions in putting this information forward.

We also did two successful programs with a doctor involved in skin care. Was this product better than any other? Were the ingredients really age controlling? Go to any pharmacy and be bedazzled by the array of products that claim the ability to turn back the clock. Most of it is utter fantasy, but the American public has always chased youth. Advertising, which is so key in our culture in setting pace and style, has always portrayed youth and vigor as the room tone for Americans who want to be noticed.

What I like is that public television has always walked in a counterclockwise fashion, offering programs at 33 rpm, when all other stations were at 45 rpm.

Yet there are moments when we cannot resist the urge to go along with the crowd. One such example, in my case, took place shortly after September 11, 2001. In that moment the nation was caught up in a frenzy of patriotic zeal. Madison Avenue has always been attuned to America's mood.

As I write this reflection on a career, we are suffering through a pandemic, and it's very interesting to see how issues of safety and caution are playing out in advertising. I can only imagine the discussions taking place around creative shops about what story to tell and what mood to strike. For instance, should all the characters in an ad be wearing a mask? Social distancing?

After 9/11, the compulsion to rally around the flag was unquenchable. Given what I said about public television, you might imagine that we held steady in designing programming to analyze, dissect, and educate the public about what had transpired; put it into historical context; and not be part of the patriotic swarm. In general, you would be right in saying that—except when it came to fundraising programming.

By this time Jim Scalem had left PBS, and Joe Campbell, the former programmer in Phoenix, took his place. We had a good relationship with him too. I credit much of that to Harriet Unger, my able and driven producer, who had designed many successful pledge events for PBS over the years. She carried the fundraising torch in ways large and small, and the system noticed.

When I was approached by a gentleman from Fairfield County, Connecticut, Don Stillman, about getting involved with a project with headliner Pat Boone, initially I balked. Pat had recorded odes to America's greatness standing in front of every piece of armament in our military arsenal. To the strains of "God Bless America," we would see the latest military aircraft soar above the rest. Really? For PBS?

It was right after 9/11. And Pat Boone, like Lawrence Welk, Andy Williams, and many others of that generation, had cache with our older viewers. Pat is a very nice man, and I enjoyed working with him.

It is fascinating to review his discography and see how he either appropriated or paid tribute—pick your description—to black music by singing songs that black artists couldn't get played in the 1950s and making them acceptable to white audiences.

I was almost hesitant to bring this project to PBS, but it was only in this moment that I could do so and not threaten my standing with them. Joe Campbell agreed to put a modest sum of money on the table to stitch these music videos together on the condition that we mount a pledge event with Pat and friends that he would assemble. Don Stillman, the consummate matchmaker and a promoter of evangelical causes, said, "Of course that would be possible."

Stillman was an enigma. He was from tony Fairfield County and was as sophisticated and charming a man as you could meet. Yet somehow he became a promoter of Christian evangelical personalities. I like and respect Don because he was a shrewd fellow, but I could not tell whether it was his faith driving him or his recognition that there was a boatload of money awaiting a dealmaker who could put projects together that would appeal to the growing faithful. I always suspected that this man who wore loafers with no socks year-round was winking his way through the whole process and collecting his cash at the window on the way out.

He introduced me to the likes of Gov. Mike Huckabee, whom Don was promoting on his book tour, and the late painter of pastoral scenes and a self-described "devout Christian," Thomas Kinkade.

Who can forget how popular Kinkade was for a time? I remember the *60 Minutes* piece in which they found collectors who literally had Thomas Kinkade galleries in their homes, rotating his work because they had run out of walls. So let me confess, in the spirit of the religiosity herein being described. I liked some of his paintings and questioned myself for doing so.

Mystery still surrounds his unexpected death in 2012—and my appreciation for his work. I just always imagined that the fewer and the rarer a painter's work, the better it was. Kinkade seemed to wake up with a paintbrush in hand and have five new ones done before his second cup of coffee.

Having gotten PBS's blessing for the Boone show, we went out to Hollywood and recorded a pledge event at the VFW Hall to make this into a plausible production. Pat Boone and I cohosted the national event. Given his smooth, comfortable style, it was a challenge to match his years of performing.

In a twist of fate, he was the national host of the Easter Seals Telethon described earlier.

Harriet Unger and I went together and were amazed at Pat's ability to gather his friends, just as he had said. There was Monty Hall, the consummate game show host from the legendary *Let's Make a Deal*; the great Red Buttons, who grew up in West Hartford, Connecticut; James Avery (I always forget his name), the guy who played the uncle on *Fresh Prince of Bel-Air*; and above all, Charlton Heston. Moses and Ben Hur were in the house, or should I say a rundown VFW building in Hollywood?

Now this was the ultimate test. I could not imagine that Charlton Heston was a big fan of PBS given his decidedly right-wing political leanings. Then again, we were all Americans in this moment.

When I presented him with a script to read about the quality of PBS documentaries, he looked at me and said something to the effect, "Aren't those all left leaning?" In my most serious tone, I responded in kind, saying, "Mr. Heston, I'm talking about Ken Burns and *The Civil War*, *American Experience*, and *National Geographic*," which were part of our offerings at the time, and he said, "Oh, all right…but…I want to read this poem."

I said, "Could I see it?"

I read through it, and it was beautiful. I asked him if he had written it.

His two-word response gave me every confidence I needed: "Robert Frost."

My own two-word response summed it all up: "Better yet."

Chapter 24: Cover Story

Television is a business of many swings and a lot of misses. If we're honest with ourselves, every business is. If you're fortunate, you can backtrack and make corrections before that faulty blueprint or bad lesson plan or program ever makes it to a recipient to judge you harshly.

I marvel at doctors and airline pilots who do not have the luxury of abject failure. On the morning of a surgery or a flight, I often wonder what might have kept them up the night before or distracted them and how they compensate for the possibility of an error that could be career- or life-threatening. In my line of work, we have often aired programs that were hastily put together or done live and had glaring problems.

Andrew Jones, having won an Emmy with our station, wanted to submit *Panama: Just Cause?* about the US incursion against Manuel Noriega for an Emmy nomination, so we both came to the station on New Year's Eve to make the deadline. The program went on the air half done while the editing process continued. We put up a graphic at the end of the completed portion saying something to the effect of "The incursion begins." That was white-knuckle theater.

Perhaps the most harrowing experience in my career came when we did a history of the University of Connecticut men's basketball team. Trying to capture a history, beginning in 1901, proved to be "a bridge too far" as my fine producer, Rich Hanley, expressed to me a few days before the broadcast. Hall of Fame coach Jim Calhoun was to be in our studio as we raised money around the show.

When he arrived, the program, still in the edit suite, hadn't even begun to touch on the coach's tenure, the most historically significant in its history, ultimately resulting in three national titles.

I was on air that night and bouncing between the edit suite and the studio, anxious as I could ever remember being in all my years of live television. No matter how many additional edit sessions I added to the schedule, we could not push the production to completion any faster. Given that we had promoted the program, what were we to do? I had to think quickly, recognizing that it was a complete embarrassment in the making live before the entire state.

I came up with a story, which I relayed to the coach and Tim Tolokan, the head of communications for UConn Athletics. Given that the production was running much longer than anticipated and that we wanted the young people in the audience to see the Calhoun portion at a reasonable hour, we would air the portions leading up to his era tonight and hold that portion until the following night.

In truth, the Calhoun era hadn't been edited at all, and we were running the earlier part of the program while putting the titling on live from the edit suite, thus further delaying the edit process. What a mess.

Mercifully, the night ended with the cover story holding. However, my producer, Rich Hanley, a wonderful freelance talent who had done some of our most popular nostalgic history programs, such as *The Flood of '55*; *Dreams Go By* about the 1965 Little League champs from Windsor Locks, Connecticut; and *The Circus Fire* about the big top fire during a circus performance in Hartford, Connecticut in 1944, had a work commitment outside CPTV the next day.

Fortunately, he was a meticulous producer and had already completed notes for the entire Calhoun segment. He left them for me and the editor, Ed Gonsalves, and we stayed all night finishing up the portion that would air the following evening. At best, all we could do with one edit session was a rough cut of the final show. Yet it aired the next night.

That final version would be packaged into a video that was being offered to our audience as a pledge incentive. It had to be sweetened, re-mixed, and packaged. The actual, complete program was not finished for about another month after it initially aired.

We had many other near misses. The most amusing was a wonderful program on phobias, which Lalia Giordano, a passionate producer, was working on. We missed one deadline after another because Lalia had a phobia about completing the program.

In television, many of your "best left undone" moments are just that. They never get completed because they are cut short for any one of a multitude of reasons—a pilot proves the talent is not right, the cost per episode is too high, your freelance producer gets called to another assignment, or funding comes in for something else—so you move along.

Nurse's Notebook was a pledge special on basic tips that you need to know for personal safety that had none of the characteristics of a successful pledge show, and it found its way in and out of schedules with the earliest reports on its dismal performance. Then there are shows that are worth doing, but the pain of the birthing process still makes it feel like a bad experience.

Our two pledge specials for PBS featuring Dr. Laura Schlessinger, then ablaze as a radio star imparting tough-as-nails psychological advice, found our scolding host none too happy about the fire alarms that woke her in the middle of the night at one of Hartford's best hotels. It happened on both visits. What are the chances?

We did a pledge special at Southern Connecticut State University with Dr. Bernie Siegel, the Yale physician who specialized in cancer treatment. He was also a pioneer in the field of mind and body connection. His books and talks were compelling. It was great content to present. However, he was legendary for his long windedness, and despite telling him that we were literally running out of tape during the production, he told the now dwindling audience, many of whom were cancer survivors, that he didn't care about the soon-to-disappear tape and that he would continue until words failed him. They rarely did.

And at a point, when we began airing University of Connecticut football games, as part of a package I will describe later, we relied on the university to tell us how much satellite time to purchase. We were new at this.

We were broadcasting a game with the University of Maine, at their home site. And they were unbound when it came to the length of their halftime festivities, where they honored every person and moose in the state, leaving us with no satellite time for the end of what turned out to be a thrilling game.

It was our *Heidi* moment, a term given to the 1968 American Football League game between the Oakland Raiders and the visiting New York Jets. The contest, held on November 17, 1968, had an exciting finish as well. Oakland scored two touchdowns in the final minute to come away victorious 43–32. However, NBC decided to break away from its coverage on the East Coast to broadcast the television movie *Heidi*. Thus, many viewers missed the Raiders' comeback.

We had some "splaining to do" trying to signal to the audience that it was our inexperience, not our intent, to deny them the final moments of the game.

There is no humiliation like public humiliation, I guess you could say.

Chapter 25: Prehistoric

Our station's involvement in national programming clearly predated my time at CPTV. Sharon Blair, my predecessor in that role, had done many projects over the years, including the previously described *Tennessee Ernie Ford's America* special.

Her biggest get was attaching the station to a new series that would become a monthly PBS staple called *Scientific American Frontiers*.

The funder, GTE, the precursor to Verizon, was headquartered in Connecticut and wanted the state public television network involved. They wanted the producers John Angier and Graham Chedd, originators of *Nova*, the preeminent science series on PBS, but did not want the heavy hand of their past employer, WGBH, in Boston.

The combination made our role as the presenting station a perfect fit. We would do all the administrative and promotion work that PBS required to make the stations happy, and Chedd and Angier, two diffident Brits, could work quietly doing the actual production work, the only phase of the business they really enjoyed.

It was a magazine series and evolved over time, hitting its stride when

Alan Alda took over as the host in the spring of 1993. He is such a fine person and actor and a devoted reader of Scientific American magazine. The series ran for fifteen years, from 1990 to 2005.

Alda was an experiential host, placing himself in the middle of new technologies. In his memoir, *Never Have Your Dog Stuffed: And Other Things I've Learned*, he recounts becoming car sick while driving a virtual reality vehicle. The taping in Chile resulted in his intestines became strangulated. He was at the top of a mountain at the time, and there was no doctor nearby. Finally they found one, and as it turns out, he was a *M*A*S*H* fan. Who wasn't?

Scientific American Frontiers was a series that CPTV was proudly associated with. Sharon did a great job of knowing how to navigate the various egos involved, including GTE's representative to the project, Mary Bryne, and Chedd-Angier, with their desire for a less-is-more presenting station. She gradually brought me into the project as she took more of a consulting role at the station.

Alan Alda gave us true star power.

Dr. Woodie Flowers, our first host, was an MIT professor and a nice man. It was the old-school model of public television programming—a professor leading his class. Alda brought a dynamism to it that set it apart. He was the avuncular uncle who did not know it all but had a wonderfully inquisitive mind and quick wit. The educational outreach component to the series was almost as important as the television production itself.

Media Management, out of Yardley, Pennsylvania, managed voluminous material distribution to schools across the country. PBS looked at the series as one that demanded no system funding and provided both educational bona fides and star power.

The educational outreach effort bridged the change in hosts. During Woodie's tenure, Sharon and Media Management put together a teleconference for education outreach people at the local PBS stations, and I had the privilege of hosting the event with him.

Sharon had me do a similar hosted event to promote another national program featuring Linda Ellerbee, the famed newswoman best known for her work on NBC and *Nick News* on Nickelodeon.

The script was all on teleprompter, and there I was coanchoring with Ms. Ellerbee, for whom I have the utmost respect. It was a pinch-me moment. After the taping, in which she made one small mistake, she looked over and smiled wryly, saying, "Hey, I'm the one who is not supposed to flub."

In the *Scientific American Frontiers* arrangement, CPTV risked nothing, was paid appropriately, and built our reputation at playing at the adults' table with our own prime-time series, albeit one that appeared monthly, not weekly.

Scientific American Frontiers would come to be known as one of three pillars of our programming stool, which ultimately gave me tremendous running room to do many of the projects that I have described in the previous chapters. It allowed me to ease into the process of managing a large, established project on PBS.

I owe Sharon Blair a great debt of gratitude, first for bringing me to CPTV as public relations manager and then showing me the ropes when it came to this type of project. The sparkle in her eye and her carefree approach to her assignments belied a steely determination to do all things her way. She carefully guarded her personal space and how she went about her business. I liked that. Sharon was not one to hang around one minute past her personal time being infringed upon. She was a past trustee of the Connecticut Humanities Council at the time that I was a new trustee. The council had their annual boat outing, and I asked Sharon how she intended to extricate herself from a situation that left few options, other than swimming back to shore. As I recall, she found a quiet place to ride out the portion of the excursion that went beyond her point of interest.

As an inheritance, *Scientific American Frontiers* was a great gift, but I wanted something I could claim as my own project. When I assumed national programming responsibilities, the system was in full-on democracy mode.

While stations begged for new programming, every time a conference was held providing new choices, the only series that got funded were the same old chestnuts. It was almost a fool's errand to offer something different. Nevertheless, this fool rushed in.

On that errand I went with a children's series called *Terrific Trips* in partnership with Cecily and Larry Lancit, owners of Lancit Media, the creators of the highly successful *Reading Rainbow*. They had done a series of field trip–type videos for Fisher-Price in the late 1980s, featuring two segments each show visiting places like aquariums, fire stations, farms, amusement parks, and the like. It was a delightful concept, well executed.

We teamed up with them to present the series to our station colleagues and, like all the other new offerings, came up short in the balloting to get system money to go forward. Breaking the code to children's programming at PBS was a monumental task. In many ways, children's programming was the holy grail.

Fred Rogers, for example, almost single-handedly saved the Corporation for Public Broadcasting's congressional appropriation when the fledging service was trying to get on its feet. PBS was born poor and had to fight for legitimacy every step of the way. In all other Western societies, the public service broadcaster was preeminent and a forerunner, such as the BBC—not an afterthought as in the United States.

Sesame Street was the top of the class and legendary in its content choices, music, Henson's character development, and New York City–based sophistication. And while PBS had the best in preschool programming with *Sesame Street* and *Mister Rogers' Neighborhood* alone, it was a struggle to find other true winners. Clearly for older children, *The Electric Company* and *Reading Rainbow* were filling huge voids.

However, PBS had adopted a mandate to serve the underserved, and preschool programming was considered not viable commercially, so the playing field was pretty much ours to fill. And Congress could justify our rather meager appropriations based on two things: that there existed a television station in virtually every congressional district and that we offered quality preschool programming.

By the time the system realized that it needed more preschool stars in its pantheon, the television landscape had changed dramatically with cable television competition. So PBS decided to scrap its overly democratized approach to a station voting process for new programs and establish a chief program executive model that would allow quicker response to the changing environment. You cannot imagine how revolutionary that model was for a system that begrudgingly gave its central command any real decision-making authority.

One of the first orders of business, directed by CPB, was the search for new preschool programming to complement our two behemoths.

Who could ever have imagined that the call that was put out for something big would be answered by a trip to a Prospect, Connecticut, video store on Super Bowl Sunday 1991?

Chapter 26: Super Bowl Sunday

William Wordsworth wrote, "The child is father of the man." There are many interpretations of that line from "My Heart Leaps Up." My own way of looking at the line is that we can learn a lot if we attempt to view an experience through a child's eyes with all the innocence and wonder of their being. As adults we have so many preexisting attitudes, biases, and prejudices that we overlook some of the simple wonders of the world. We often imagine that complexity connotes value and purpose when a simple minute watching the flight of a hummingbird or walking and admiring a babbling brook on a fall day may be more enriching and soul-inspiring than any of the activities to which we ascribe greater value.

On Super Bowl Sunday 1991, I had a checklist of activities I needed to do to feel fulfilled. Knowing me, I needed to jog, play my drums, and probably go through a stack of work that I brought home and then watch "The Game." That was when I still watched football.

That day our four-year-old daughter, Leora, who had passing interest in television, wanted to go to the Prospect Video Store on the main road in our little town. Coming from her, it was an unusual request, but it was certainly one way to idle the day.

Among the rather limited offerings for children was a video titled *Barney and the Backyard Gang*, the video forerunner to Barney the Dinosaur on television. It seemed perfectly fine as a video distraction for her. The episode was "A Day at the Beach."

We brought the video home, and since in those days an adult was needed to rewind the VHS and start it again, it became apparent to me that she was really taken with this program. She asked to see it time and again.

I decided to stop whatever I was doing and see what was fascinating her. What I saw was rather rudimentary from a production standpoint—the lighting gave Barney a somewhat menacing look to be honest; the voice deeper than you might recall; and the pacing slower than is common, even in a program meant to be less vignette driven and more continuous in its story line.

There was one adult in the video, Sandy Duncan, who had a role. But as I recall, she gave much of the adult supervisory responsibility to Barney.

As I settled in to watch, I was mindful that PBS and CPB had recently put out a call to system producers indicating that they were looking to fund a few new projects to add to the preschool lineup. The feeling was that we needed reinforcements for *Sesame Street* and *Mister Rogers' Neighborhood* to keep young children watching PBS. The research showed that cable networks were impacting our franchise because it was typical for younger children, our crowd, to "watch up." An older sibling controlled the viewing, and preschool children followed their lead.

Millions of dollars were set aside for a competition in which the system would put one season of three new series on the air and, based upon performance, settle on one or perhaps two series that would go into ongoing production.

Did this mean a lot to CPTV? Not really. Truthfully we were not a player in that sense.

Anyone looking to enter this competition had to imagine that the active development shops at behemoths such as WNET in New York and WGBH in Boston, or Children's Television Workshop, or another outside producer of children's programming would take the bait and spend some real time and money preparing for the next big thing.

Earlier I stated that our dictate to play in the national programming game was clear—avoid spending money you don't have and take on projects that are in some stage of development. We looked to find programs in an emerging phase, which allowed us to play a role in their production and add value but not assume risk.

As I plopped down on the couch to watch what was getting so much mindshare from my daughter that day, I saw a lead character who seemed loving and open to children. Barney was not as neurotic as Big Bird. The program moved at a gentle pace that could be calming to a young child, employed a set and use of color, and that while less than highly professional, had promise and familiar and catchy music underpinning the entire production.

I was not a children's programming producer, I remind you.

If you started at the beginning of this book, I made clear the many unfamiliar situations that cast me in roles that I seemed to be less than fully prepared for. Perhaps the ability to don a disguise and surprise both myself and others was a big part of the thrill of it all.

A focus group of one was clearly not enough to go to experienced children's program evaluators and demand a king's ransom. Larry Rifkin? CPTV? What? It was truly implausible, but then again that improbability dots the landscape of the new and unimagined.

While I have shuttled and time-shifted various aspects of my life in this telling, this Barney sighting came along just a few years after the acquisition of a lot of Emmy Awards in Boston in 1989.

Our coming of age as a regional producer of quality programs constituted what I considered a high-water mark. It symbolized about all I could imagine accomplishing from my perch in an old station facility on the Trinity College campus in the south end of Hartford, Connecticut. Never did I imagine that I would end up trying to manage one of the greatest success stories in the history of American children's television.

And yet there I was fumbling to find the video box, so I could see who produced this nascent program. I saw the name Sheryl Leach and decided to give her a call on Monday.

Chapter 27: Barney before PBS

Call it an epiphany of sorts or just the desperate attempt by a frazzled mother to find some way to occupy the time of her hard-to-please two-year-old son.

Sheryl knew that keeping it simple and giving young children a loving character, a bold palette of colors, and catchy songs, with age-appropriate learning moments sprinkled throughout, was all that was needed to achieve success.

In Sheryl Leach's case, she harkened back to growing up loving wholesome programs such as *Romper Room*, *Sky King*, *The Mickey Mouse Club*, and *Our Gang*. As a former elementary school teacher with a master's degree in bilingual education, her thoughts were often on stimulating the mind of the young child.

With a specific child in mind, she was rolling down the Central Expressway in Dallas one day in 1987, and her fertile mind was focused on finding something her son, Patrick, would watch that would hold his attention. And what started out as a snuggly teddy bear that came to life and interacted with children became a purple dinosaur named Barney.

Leora letting the world know Barney was coming to PBS almost a year before the TV launch on Friday, June 28, 1991 photo credit: Michael Asaro, Republican-American

The metamorphosis in her thinking came about as a traveling dinosaur exhibit rolled into town, and Patrick's passion for the extinct creatures was front and center in her mind. While bigger and scarier than teddy bears, the fact that they no longer roamed the earth made the interaction more fantastical and less foreboding to a child. And Sheryl made sure that her dinosaur had soft edges and bore no resemblance to what later would inhabit, say, Jurassic Park.

As luck would have it, Sheryl's father-in-law, Richard Leach, had just expanded his printing operation, located on the outskirts of Dallas in a town called Allen, with a production studio. Sheryl, in her persuasive way, convinced Richard that she; Kathy Parker, another former teacher; and Dennis DeShazer, video producer, could find use for that studio by doing home videos featuring her children's character.

Sheryl and Kathy did much research in the process by attempting to find holes in the existing marketplace of children's videos. They watched everything they could find to determine, based on their own understanding of the developing brains of preschoolers, what elements they needed in such offerings.

They knew that meeting the emotional, cognitive, and motor development needs of children, in combination, was not only the right formula for educational success but would also yield commercial bounty to the producers who could find the right balance. And despite little experience in video production, they were confident they could accomplish those objectives.

With an ensemble of local children in the neighborhood, they started making *Barney and the Backyard Gang* home videos.

Concomitant with their savvy on the programming side was a keen marketing sense as to how to get these videos seen using guerilla tactics given a nonexistent advertising budget. They purchased a mailing list of three thousand toy and gift stores and recruited a corps of Barney moms, otherwise known as their friends and later as mom blitzers, to get the word out about these shows that enchanted young children.

In what they called Operation Preschool, they sent out free tapes to these centers to get buzz about what they were originating in Dallas.

While it may sound contrived to look out the rearview mirror having created the rage of an era and emphatically say no, Sheryl has repeatedly given that response when asked whether she had any doubt that Barney would be a hit with preschoolers.

Having gotten to know her over many years, this is not balderdash. She was confident from the beginning that what she and her team were building would be a success.

The nine early videos they produced won the Parents' Choice Award and other competitions. They began building an associated product line that found its way into Neiman Marcus catalogs and Barney boutiques.

The Barney idea was taking on some traction. It was, by no means, at this point a national sensation. That would follow once Sheryl came to the phone when I rang her up in 1991.

Chapter 28: The Phone Call

My phone call found a willing recipient on the other end. Sheryl Leach, I would come to discover, was confident in the vision she had for her video property, Barney. She was the progenitor who was wise enough to bring along others she trusted to help her realize her vision.

Like many other creators and originators, she would guard jealously the carefully designed creature of her own making. Every new entreaty from an outside entity had to set off some alarm bells, cautioning Sheryl to be very wary of their motives.

Later on I would know the feeling. After bringing Barney to the pinnacle of success on PBS and in the general culture, I was beseeched with requests from others who felt passionately that they had created the next big thing.

It was somewhat ironic that I became the person who had to ask them the hard questions about what they loved most about their children's property and wonder what motive they had in coming to me. If they said, as one woman from Ohio did, that she loved putting on live events in her hometown and seeing the faces of the children light up when her characters came to life, I told her to save money for the plane ticket to Hartford to see me and enjoy the simplicity and uncomplicated experience for what it is.

I can assure you that when a passion becomes a business, complications set in. Egos become more fragile, and often hard business considerations turn what was once joy into painful choices. All that was in the future.

On this call, it was all about hopes, expectations, and dreams. Sheryl listened for a bit and said, "PBS, tell me more." So as limited as my realm of experience was in the children's arena, to her I was an authority on the PBS system.

Why would I let on that CPTV had no children's properties and that, for all I knew, this entire testing process might already have been inside tracked for all the usual suspects? It was the kind of foreplay that goes on all the time in television before the whole thing gets scrapped and you move on to the next project.

If you do not like dead ends and blind alleys, then television program development is not for you. There are more pitches that end up coming up short than at most peewee league baseball games.

Given that a wink is as good as a nod to a blind horse and that I am a convincing presenter of hope and possibility, Sheryl agreed to continue the conversation and let me guide the way through a system she knew virtually nothing about.

What I sensed from Sheryl was a resolute confidence that she would entertain such a possibility without cordoning off others that might come her way. She was too shrewd to do that. After all, she had already undertaken successful development and production of a home video series against the backdrop of little experience and family politics, which might have deterred someone of less strong will. She also had lots of ideas about the marketing of her property and used the Dallas area to test out those concepts.

I figured that if none of this worked out, perhaps I could make some extra cash on the side by getting the franchise to run Barney parties in Connecticut. Really, I did.

Let me fast-forward and answer the question, which surely is on your mind, as to whether I became rich from my role in this phenomenon. In any traditional commercial undertaking, I would have been entitled to millions. However, the answer is no. CPTV, in the seventeen years of our coproduction relationship, found financial stability in the many millions it earned. In the process, I solidified my position there, thus allowing me to make a good living and continue in a dream job. That was what was most important to me. I took the public broadcasting ethos very seriously and felt that it was my role to benefit appropriately but not profit indiscriminately. My wife disagrees and thinks that I undervalued my centrality in all that took place.

Growing up with my talented dad who made, I believe, $12,500 at his earning peak, in what I thought was the best job in the world meant that I never equated dollars with satisfaction. In fact, while Jerry Franklin valued the cash cow he had and would bonus me regularly, I often shared it with indispensable staff. Key among them was my longtime assistant, Lisa Di Donato Cambria. I called her my human prophylactic as she was my front-facing eyes and ears to the world and would protect me against any incoming she judged to be malign. With her salty and uproarious mouth and engaging personality, she became an extension of me. She was smart, sassy, and clearly in sync with where each project was in each stage of its development.

In the spirit of truth telling, Lisa and I had over a quarter century of good years together, but in that sweep, we had one bad year. I cannot recall exactly why that was, but like any long relationship, we were not meshing in that season.

It came later in my tenure at CPTV when I felt that all my important work there was done, but I had no place to go and did not want to live with the ghosts of past success. I could not compete. I felt like I was out of place and time.

However, in 1991, and with this call, little did I know that I was on the verge of writing my own ticket for years to come.

Sheryl and I agreed to continue exploring the situation with no unrealistic expectations. I was an honest broker and made clear to her that I was a program executive at one station, by no means the final decision-maker, and that we had to agree to proceed with full knowledge that this was a long shot.

Fortunately, the open call for new series was not a charade and had not been predetermined. That is not to say that prejudices about players and properties would not quickly be formed and that early buy-in might give way to later turmoil.

The Barney story is anything but a straight line, yet I was blessed to be on the jagged edge of what turned out to be one of a handful of true children's programming hits that redefined the genre and created new copycats and competitors looking to recreate the inexplicable magic.

I have said many times that had Sheryl, Kathy Parker, and Dennis DeShazer not started with a desire to design a character with true educational value for preschoolers and instead made it all about a shameless money grab, I would never have been able to ward off the many critics of Barney inside and outside the system.

Nothing I had ever done before could truly prepare me for what would unfold.

Chapter 29: Barney, Shari, and Shining Time Station

While I do not imagine myself a "new age" thinker, I like a range of thought and was open to presenting it as a public television content gatekeeper.

Isn't that the mission of public television, to let new voices and ideas be heard?

That notion was put to the test when CPTV, along with the Connecticut Arts Commission, sponsored a film and video competition, and Elda Hartley, a longtime producer of shows about "new age" thinkers, entered a short film. Lo and behold, this very experienced hand, with her own film foundation, was a winner of the contest. We then struck up a respectful relationship as she proposed we work together on what would come to be *Voices of the New Age*, featuring thinkers like Ram Dass, Jean Houston, John White, and others.

I take this detour to accent the point that often the greater the risk, the bigger the reward.

In working with Elda, I wondered whether she would listen to an executive producer whose inexperience was profound in comparison with her years in the business. As it turned out, rough cut after rough cut, with comments I made, she dutifully responded with new material. She never questioned my judgment and made each succeeding cut better than the last until we had a program that I was proud to represent to programming colleagues across the country.

Elda and I were so different from each other, and yet I was so impressed that she let me share in her creative vision for the project with deference and humility. In many ways I can say the same thing of Sheryl Leach. While self-confidence and shrewdness were part of her makeup, so was an abiding faith in her ability to read situations. After a certain number of phone calls and relaying my best understanding of the situation that faced us going forward, she sensed that we could share this experience in a harmonious way despite our different skill sets and backgrounds. That was a testament to her faith, not so much in me but in the work to this point that made such a call possible.

I later came to realize how her equanimity in the face of distressing news made her a great role model to me. She demonstrated the ability to stare down failure and not succumb to it as an essential ingredient in all business affairs. More to that point shortly. First, we had to win, place, or show.

PBS and CPB had to settle on three finalists for this on-air competition to take our place in the pantheon of PBS children's programming, alongside *Sesame Street* and *Mister Rogers' Neighborhood*.

In a sense, all the folks at PBS and CPB had to do was come out with one clear winner, bat .333, which is doable, and their job was a success. If two out of the three resonated with audiences, all the better. We had a whole lot of selling to do to make it into this group of finalists. After all, if CPTV was a distant relative to this national children's competition and PBS's most cherished program franchise, Sheryl's team could not be found anywhere on the family tree.

Sheryl represented the Lyons Group, and they produced their videos in Allen, Texas, which is well on the outskirts of Dallas. At the time it was in the middle of nowhere for all intents and purposes. It would be a leap of faith for PBS and CPB to take a chance on an inexperienced station and even more unknown producing partner to surmount the objections they would throw in our path.

Do you have the producing capability to go from zero to sixty in producing thirty episodes in a year's time? Do you have the financial wherewithal to make up for any shortfalls in your budget since you will only be given a percentage of the direct costs?

More critical for their consideration of the series was whether we, indeed, were worthy creatively and educationally to carry the PBS banner.

After all, we only had a handful of videos, which as I said were aspirational but not conclusive as to what this property could become. The production was in its infancy. It still required a leap of imagination to stand up to the rigors of scrutiny from PBS programmers, critics, and those producers who were already respected and tested in the children's realm. We would come to see all those constituencies as challenges going forward.

While some of the specifics in terms of number of meetings, calls, and various interactions required to press our case are lost in the canyon of time, I do recall that much of what I had responsibility for had to be set aside to allow for the process to play itself out.

It was a process in which much about our relationship with the Lyons Group would come into greater focus as we went back and forth over the many necessary accommodations.

The name of the series itself had to change. The videos were *Barney and the Backyard Gang*. PBS might do a documentary special on the gangs of LA, but it would have none of that in the title of a children's series.

Barney himself would be the surrogate adult. There was no need for Sandy Duncan.

What kind of cast of children could you come up with in the Dallas, Texas, area? Would they be talented enough as characters in the production? Are your facilities up to our standard? What kind of money would be required to make it so?

CPTV had to convince PBS that it would be a true coproducing partner, assuring the system that what resulted would not be substandard on any level. While we would send cameras and people down to Texas to offer advice and support, PBS had to wonder whether our expertise was really that which could assure the patina and cover for any of their myriad concerns.

One of PBS's key concerns was the commercial torque behind the program from the beginning. While Sheryl and Kathy, as preschool educators, came at this having scoured the video marketplace to determine what had been missing in all that was available to this audience, the goal was a commercial success on some level.

Fortunately, they started with the premise that an educational foundation is what children need to become deeply immersed with the character because at this age learning is fun, engaging, and the bedrock of sustainable success.

From the established benchmarks that children's television watchdog, Peggy Charren, might use to judge the validity of a program's efficacy, perhaps the more instinctive and comparative approach Sheryl and Kathy took was not up to her standards. Charren's watchdog group, Action for Children's Television, was always on the lookout for a commercial interest getting its nose under the PBS tent. In her mind, I would imagine, the commercial networks were hopeless in this regard, and her only oasis on the dial was PBS.

If PBS sponsored and fostered a thinly veiled *Care Bears*–type property for the sake of ratings and pledge viability, the battle was lost. This kind of concern clearly had to weigh on PBS and CPB's mind in the process.

It is helpful to note the two other series funded under this call. One was *Lamb Chop's Play-Along!* with ventriloquist and children's entertainer Shari Lewis, reprising a role for her most famous puppet. Its presenting station was WTTW in Chicago.

Shari Lewis came on to the scene originally having won the first prize on the CBS television series *Arthur Godfrey's Talent Scouts* in 1952. Shortly thereafter, she had her own series and was engaged in games, songs, stories, and craft-making to delight children and adults alike. Her network debut took place on NBC in 1960, featuring her many characters—Hush Puppy, Charlie Horse, Wing Ding, and Lamb Chop—which basically consisted of little more than a sock with eyes. Produced in Canada decades later, the series allowed Shari Lewis to bring her cast of characters to PBS. The series would ultimately run for four seasons after being green-lighted for an initial package of twenty-nine episodes, starting on January 13, 1992.

The other series selected was presented by WNET in New York. *Shining Time Station*, an American series, was jointly created by Britt Allcroft, from Britain, and Rick Siggelkow, an American television producer. The series was an amalgam, incorporating segments from the British television series *Thomas & Friends*. Those sequences were based on Rev. Wilbert Awdry's books, *The Railway Series*. And while the series starred Ringo Starr as Mr. Conductor, as the storyteller in a limited runback in 1989, a gifted comedian, George Carlin, assumed the role in 1991 and maintained it through its end in 1995.

PBS and CPB funded this series, as part of the call, to see if it could put more money behind a well-supported *Shining Time Station*, which could become a staple on American television. *Thomas & Friends* later emerged on its own, apart from its introduction in the United States as part of *Shining Time Station*.

Of the other two properties vying for long-term viability on PBS with the newly titled *Barney & Friends*, Shari Lewis seemed to take the fight for permanence more personally and showed her disdain for us in various ways.

We were underestimated from birth.

While our true fans, the audience, were too small to speak up for us, their parents who lost their children in the land Barney created for them often rued our being. In the mix of issues at the time, Shari had a fan base built of a generation of parents and television critics who grew up loving her and her characters. If they were picking a winner, clearly it was her and not us.

Shining Time Station had the gravitas of coming from literature and Britain too—a perfect pairing for public television. And there was a certain star appeal with Ringo and then George Carlin.

There we were, Allen, Texas, meets Hartford, Connecticut, to develop an unholy alliance to take PBS over the commercial divide with what many believed was saccharin. Who would have bet on that?

In a measured way and with a wary eye, somehow PBS and CPB did, allotting us $2.5 million to produce thirty episodes in about a year's time. We were the last entry in this children's sweepstakes to hit the air on April 6, 1992. The PBS sign-off came from then children's director, Jeff Gabel.

The year in development was time enough for Jeff Gabel, who also ushered *Where in the World Is Carmen Sandiego?* and *The Magic School Bus* on to PBS, to have left his post. As Chuckles the Clown, he appeared as a special guest on *Mister Rogers' Neighborhood* in 1986.

Without a true advocate at PBS and with hungry and established competitors and many question marks surrounding our origins and intentions, a star was born in a constellation of doubt.

Chapter 30: The Curious Ride

If elation and trepidation can coexist, it was living in the house of Larry after the green light was given to start the rebuild of the Barney franchise into a PBS-worthy property.

So much had to be done against an almost impossible deadline, which you only agree to because you have no choice. And you trust that money can solve any problems yet unimagined along the way. As I look back, it is a bit surprising that the field of entries came down to the three of us.

The public television system had waited a long time to enhance the preschool lineup, and at the end of the day, a British-based literary offering, a past-prime American commercial television puppeteer, and this funny-looking dinosaur with the goofy voice were what remained.

Programmers across the country wished us luck as we were a new system player in the mix with a totally untested property, but I could tell they imagined that this effort to blunt the impact of the cable universe was like trying to hold back a raging river with a matchstick dam. Did I know something others did not? In truth, no.

What if the Lyons Group's homespun research, more gut than empirical, led to a false conclusion about the merits of the property? What if my daughter and others we enlisted to sample the product turned out to be the only living boys and girls in America to like what they saw?

I guess I would relate back to the old Henny Youngman joke about the guy who hears a voice telling him to go back to Las Vegas and bet on red number seven. He goes back, bets on red number seven, and loses, and the voice says, "How 'bout that?"

Sorry, guys, my bad.

I really did not have time to envision such failure. I was too wrapped up in imagining all the work ahead to give success a chance. And fretting, at what point, the project would go off the rails, thanks to my inexperience or the lack of familiarity of our partners with the enormity of the task at hand.

There were legal relationships to establish, production elements to set in place, a functioning unit in Texas to support and enhance, and the need to constantly attempt to act as a translator and ambassador with my portfolio to make clear how different it was producing for PBS as opposed to home video distribution or even a commercial network.

In the process, while a major consideration was protecting against a downside risk that the Lyons Group's inexperience might require CPTV to get involved in a bailout if they could not deliver on the budget provided, perhaps I should have focused more on the upside potential.

Did I undervalue the enormity of the pot of gold at the end of the Barney rainbow? I was always a calculated rainmaker. I did not want to overplay my hand. Remember the $10,000 pacesetter gift from Timex for my first Easter Seals Telethon? Prestige and purpose guided me as much as profit.

After all, here I was trying to keep our partners from killing the golden goose because of their propensity to market aggressively. Would I choose to share in any recklessness that might be seen in this if we were waiting for many of those spoils to flow to us?

I did want title to the developing series, so we signed on, not only as a presenting station, a more administrative and promotional duty, but also as a coproducer.

Even the legal counsel we each had was representative of our thrust in this.

We retained Atty. Malcolm Stevenson of Schwartz, Woods & Miller, a firm that basically did Washington-based work for public television clients. His domain was more the rulebook of FCC requirements than a major production deal. He became a wonderful friend and advisor, who was focused on ensuring we all stayed within the public television boundaries.

It is difficult to minimize our inexperience in these matters particularly when juxtaposed with the fact that we were bringing an aggressive for-profit partner into the realm of the most coveted and protected realm of the nonprofit PBS universe. Add to this the fact that no one could imagine that we would be dealing with a once-in-a-generation smash hit that would test all norms.

Tom Gherardi, former attorney at CPB, was hired by our coproducing partners. He had a flair for the spoken word and a dramatic flourish. He loved the sound of his own voice. In a way we all enjoyed his playful soliloquies as he lectured us on a range of issues with each subsection of the agreement we would negotiate.

CPTV came away with a good deal, but the value of our contribution was immeasurable.

While Dennis DeShazer personalized the issue by reminding me in a phone call recently, "Without you, the Barney phenomenon does not take place," I was a representative of CPTV, and its role was invaluable throughout.

We received 30 percent of the net share of goods sold for pledge purposes within the public television system and home video sales derived from the PBS production, both to be split between CPTV and PBS, as well as a production and representation budget for services rendered on behalf of the series. We were also incentivized to find underwriting monies and retain a portion.

On the commercial side, the range of Barney products remained exclusively the domain of the Lyons Group, and they were masterful in holding on to video rights, which they could directly market rather than just accepting a royalty from a major distributor. The difference in that one move alone represented probably $5 or more on each video. Can you imagine?

This was one of the great challenges for me throughout this process. No matter how many times I pleaded with our partners not to sell too many licenses for low-end Barney goods, such stuff kept showing up in the marketplace, and I had to answer to PBS about it.

In all fairness, some of this stuff was not of their making. Pirate product was showing up everywhere and lending impetus to the oversaturation. How many horrible Barney-suited impostors showed up at birthday parties around the country?

We could become a flash in the pan, or we could strive to nurture a long-term, classic property that would bring value for generations. In some sense, we ended up with a hybrid, which makes the Barney story even more unique.

I always believed in the values and educational richness of the series. I just had to prove it to a range of skeptics.

While we were always chasing legitimacy throughout our seventeen years associated with the breakout hit of a generation, so, too, were we required to amplify the still, small voices of our fans to drown out the din of naysayers betting on, and hoping for, the demise of the purple dinosaur.

Chapter 31: Orphaned at Birth

If you are like me, your greatest excitement is the anticipation of receiving something, not the actual retrieval of the item or thing. Often that is something of a letdown.

If it is a new bit of technology, for example, you wait days for it to arrive, and then when it does, there are a host of duties you do not look forward to—figuring out how it works, ways to transfer information from the older version, where to put the instruction manual, how to process the warranty, and even how to dispose the gear replaced.

The yearlong buildup to Barney's debut was a wonderful year in that sense.

Whether this series was a success, our station getting a $2.5 million grant from PBS and CPB was historic. Our entry in the children's domain was monumental. The sense of possibility, even if our hope of prevailing in this competition might seem remote, was energizing. It was a year of consequence. Not a day or a week but a full year to imagine and hope.

By now, given what you know about me, I attacked this span of time with everything I had.

Looking back, I am sure I left my incredibly capable wife with even more of the responsibility of raising our children, then five and eight. She was also handed the responsibility of incorporating the added assistance my mother, Edith, needed as she fought misdiagnosed stage four uterine cancer. At the outset of her long journey, the doctors thought it was ovarian cancer and thus operated on her without removing her uterus. In fact, the surgeon at the time suggested if it were his mother, he would give up on her. Thankfully, with the gift of a tenacious partner, we did just the opposite and joined my mother's war to fight back for seven years.

As much as my wife is a copilot on Rifkin Air, I look back and marvel at her willingness to let me do what I had to do to see this project to the finish line given her growing set of professional and personal responsibilities.

This process involved repeatedly shuttling back and forth from Connecticut to Texas and many trips to deal with business and creative issues in Washington, DC, and at PBS headquarters in Alexandria, Virginia. I would say 70 percent of my time was spent at work dealing with this one project. Everything else had to take a back seat.

Fortunately, this is when you find out how good your team is and what goodwill you have banked along the way.

Lisa Di Donato Cambria's singular importance in ensuring everyone who needed my attention felt that by having her word, she would get to me on something while I was Barney-involved proved invaluable.

Andrea Hanson, our most capable and well-respected program director, responsible for the crafting of our schedule and acquisitions, was a steady hand throughout. She had great maturity and focus and was respected throughout the PBS system. Knowing that Andrea was always tending to the more unrelenting tasks of keeping the programming ship afloat allowed me to play free safety in finding and then nurturing new possibilities. We were a synchronous unit.

If you are the dealmaker in your organization, you need that kind of infrastructure in place so that should you land Moby Dick, you have crew members who can handle a myriad of other duties while your gaze is fixed.

I truly wish I could rewind the clock and savor the level of expectation, tinged with fear of failure, that the period between April 1991 and April 1992 represented in my life. I might have been too singularly focused on checklist after checklist of the immediate tasks at hand to enjoy the thirty-thousand-foot ride that this was.

Sometimes great opportunities come your way, and the gestation period is short. Decide now, or let it slip away. Here I had a runway moment that allowed me to glide into this launch, and while my head should have been up, more times than not, it was down.

The only moments I could sit back and reflect, without the benefit of immediate pressures, were on my flights to and from Texas. There were no digital gadgets to distract; no one else was with me. I was truly alone. Most times in the past, when I traveled on business for CPTV, Andrea and I would go together and have great times talking about a range of topics, often politics.

While she was more progressive than me on a range of issues, I was the political moderate who tried to keep the editorial ship as steady as possible, lest the sense that public television was a left-leaning enterprise would be validated in many people's eyes.

If you understand the state of Connecticut, the land of steady habits, we are not a deep blue state. We are light blue and have never had trouble electing moderate Republicans, such as Sen. Lowell Weicker, Rep. Chris Shays, and Gov. John Rowland.

That was when Republicans could get elected in New England. Each party's ideological purity mitigates against that today. Thus, what were intraparty squabbles, resolved before approaching the other side with a position already moderated by compromise, are now pitched battles between two parties that have been rinsed of internal debate.

While I was about to launch a career-defining enterprise, at heart my love and passion was as a Connecticut guy, a Waterbury guy, who had the keys to the candy store of the most exciting editorial shop I could have ever imagined. That would have been enough for me. Connecticut is a small state, and such a position allows you to have a sizable impact.

While I mentioned my dabbling in politics as a young man, in that process I got to know John Rowland, another Waterbury guy, who later became governor, a Waterbury Republican no less, who was elected to the office three times. He later fell into disgrace and did two terms in prison. More on that later.

While I was and am a Democrat, in a city John inhabited comfortably even under a different political label, the fact that we were both from Waterbury was a greater assignation of our being.

When he first ran for Congress, he phoned me and asked if I would write his first political speech for federal office. I said, "John, our views are a bit different." He said something along the lines of "Yeah, I know, but just write me something to help me get going." I recall making him so liberal it took him the entire primary campaign against his opponent, Alan Schlessinger, to get back to the right. He called it his "Ted Kennedy speech."

While John was governor, Waterbury's star shone bright in the state capitol. It was almost cool to be from downtrodden Waterbury. You couldn't watch a hearing in Hartford without seeing a Waterbury person chairing the committee of record.

When CPTV needed to convert from analogue to digital broadcasting, John Rowland put $10 million into his capital budget for the conversion. And while I credit most of that to Jerry Franklin's aggressive lobbying, there is a part of me that says having a Waterbury guy in the lead programming chair was also a part of his thinking. Maybe even the speech that launched, and almost sunk, his political career before it got started had something to do with it.

No matter how many plane rides and flights of fancy on national projects I took, I was happily tethered to this place. This place owned my heart.

Throughout my tenure at CPTV, I served as vice chair of the State Commission on Children (thanks, Barney) and as a member of the state's Film and Video Commission and, as previously mentioned, the Connecticut Humanities Council.

I had some pangs of remorse that so much of my time was now on a singular mission with no guarantee that the investment in time would result in a successful outcome. As I introduced friends and family to what I was working on, there were quizzical looks as to whether I was on a fool's errand.

As the Barney saga unfolded, I fumbled through this dream sequence with few disagreements with our partners, except on the issue of aggressive marketing of the developing phenom. This is worth pointing out because that level of accommodation and the synchronicity of our mutual goodwill throughout was key to our survival as the gathering headwinds began to push against us.

I liked the principals involved—Sheryl, Kathy, and Dennis—and appreciated each for what they brought to the table. When I needed to understand the long-term direction of the project, I would turn to Sheryl; when I needed to understand an educational aspect of the project, I could turn to Kathy and her protégé, Mary Ann Dudko, PhD; and when I needed to confer on a production element, Dennis was always there. While Sheryl and Dennis remain close to this day, the threesome would part ways as the saga unfolded.

It is hard to imagine it would unfold in any other way given the stakes involved, the family involvement, and the pressures of turning a seed corn into a cash dinosaur.

We worked through issue after issue with confidence in what we were about to bring to the nation. I was pleased at how well the gears of the production machine in Texas accommodated the PBS requirement to enhance every aspect of the production from sets to lighting to sound.

Even the process of finding and hiring child actors in the heart of Texas went well. I was impressed that the state had work rules for children that were as exacting as they were. Selena Gomez and Demi Lovato are two stars who got their start in the series. Others have gone on to fine careers in the arts too. The Lyons Group tended to these special talents by developing a school program for them on set.

My most vivid recollection in the lead up to our launch was our coming-out party. We were invited to California for the twice-yearly media gaggle, known as the TV press tour, to introduce television critics to new shows coming in the season ahead.

To say that the expectations on this untested property were low was clearly an understatement. They were nonexistent.

Most of the television writers were middle-aged white men who really had no idea what made this series work. They not only dismissed us after our presentation with very few questions, but they also canonized Shari Lewis because they grew up loving her.

If there were a betting pool in that room, everyone there would have lost their shirts. It feels good to say that.

Much has been written in this period about the death of expertise. Given this Trumpian notion, I do not want to contribute to the foolhardy nature of that assertion.

It is the reason when I walk into an airplane, I feel confident I am going to land in one piece. It is the reason that the many times I've gone under for surgery, I could imagine nothing less than reemerging whole and better. However, I have tried to admit in this recollection that in some fields—like my own—there is little certainty that your judgment will translate into popular appeal. I'm struck lately in looking for a score on Rotten Tomatoes to find how often critics and the public disagree on the appeal of a film. It is the reason I could never review Hallmark movies during Christmas season. What do I know about the appeal? I don't watch them. Please ask my wife. She does and likes them.

Then again, I did not see any three-year-old children with pens and pads in that press gathering. They were not represented.

At the time Jim Endrst was the capable and probing television columnist for the *Hartford Courant*. He and I had a combative but respectful relationship. While he recognized the changing nature of CPTV in my time there as evidenced by some glowing reviews of the heightened output and good storytelling, I knew he preferred the glitz of commercial television.

Owen McNally, who preceded Jim at the *Hartford Courant*, liked nothing more than to devour a ten-part series of *Masterpiece Theatre*. I do not recall that English fare being Jim's cup of tea. He was at the press event introducing Barney but not in the room when we presented. Mind you, this was our hometown paper, and CPTV was launching the most important project of its existence.

Jim and I recently went back and forth about this on social media. He said that he had access to me whenever he wanted, knew the property well, and had no need to be there. In the scheme of things, it was emblematic of the way we were, from the beginning, not considered anything resembling a sure thing. And in fairness they had no reason to understand the power of Barney. Unlike *Sesame Street*, it made no pretense of entertaining children and adults.

Few understood what kind of vacuum existed for the three- and four-year-old crowd on television. They were underserved for a reason. First, it was believed that they could not move merchandise accompanying a series, and second, there were many who believed that we should not consciously program to that age group because they should be doing more tactile, less passive things.

I can understand the latter argument. It falls apart, however, when you realize that children will watch the tube with their older siblings if there is nothing there for them. Watching up, as it is called, is like dressing younger children in the older child's hand-me-downs before they are ready for them.

Let's just say that there was pent-up demand for the needs that Barney would address. When you provide children with content that is age appropriate and responsive to their emotional and educational needs, well, you have Barney. So we became the "other" early on.

While I could accept the lack of awareness of what I just said on the part of the media, it was harder to accept from our new program chieftains at PBS.

To have just celebrated launch day, and to be told that you were an orphan at birth, rejected before you had your turn, was all too much.

Chapter 32: The Mania Wins

The maxim that success has many fathers and failure is an orphan is true.

It seems like anyone who put their hand on the Barney hot stove in the early 1990s felt the heat, and some glowed in response, and others quickly backed away at the time.

By the time we were ready to debut in April 1992, the original green-lighter for children's programming at PBS was gone. The old system of voting for programs was scuttled, and authority to make decisions was vested in a chief programming executive. While Jennifer Lawson, the first person to occupy that role, had been in place since 1989, this call for a new preschool series was not something she engaged in directly.

I believe it was a wait-and-see proposition as PBS and CPB went about the initial evaluation process. There were no specific metrics to determine whether a series would be allowed a new lease on life after the test. The system would know success when they saw it. Or would they? After this full year of development and meeting unreal deadlines with a much-improved Barney property, I approached this moment with great anticipation.

It was Monday, April 6, 1992.

In that year leading up to the debut, a moment of great pride was bringing Barney to Oakdale Musical Theatre in Wallingford, Connecticut. At the time it was still an open-air tent with a stage in the round.

I had enjoyed so many wonderful memories there, thanks to Ben and his son, Beau Segal, who gave Connecticut a magical stage experience in the allowing seasons of the year. It was amazing to watch performers figure out how to work their acts as they twirled around. Don Rickles used it as a prop, telling stagehands to stop because he was getting seasick, and Harry Chapin played to each quadrant of the audience as he went by as if it were a new audience to dazzle and charm.

My dad had been very friendly with Ben Segal, and he would bring me autographs of performers he met at Oakdale. The one that meant the most, and yet caused some embarrassment, was Dave Clark of the Dave Clark Five. As the group that competed with the Beatles at the outset as best band from Britain, having the autograph made me want to stand on the side of the DC5 as being better than the Beatles. I pled that case with Steve Mednick until it became too untenable to assert any longer.

My most interesting backstage moment at Oakdale was in the early 1980s and involved the country star Minnie Pearl and her husband. She agreed to do a promo for a series we had purchased called "Classic Country," which consisted of vintage Grand Ole Opry performances from the 1950s. It was a throw-in with a package of *National Geographic Specials* offered by Gannaway Entertainment.

Evidently the performers, such as Ms. Pearl, were never given royalties to the material, and yet there it was still making money for the distributor decades later. Her husband was about to throw me and the crew out of her dressing room when he realized what we were there for. Ms. Pearl calmed him down and said that it wasn't my fault. She agreed to record the spots.

Being here at this auspicious moment in my career called up a host of

*Leora and Barney at CPTV studios,
June, 1992*

feelings about this place. And on this day, it was rocking with toddlers. We attracted a full house with the word of mouth about the upcoming series, CPTV's role in it, and availability of early home videos, which we aired in advance.

The Barney body actor, David Joyner, a muscular guy who brought joy to the complicated movements of the character in this suffocating costume, and Bob West, the unmistakable voice for the character, who resided outside the body, brought their talents to the event.

The girl responsible for the find, my daughter, Leora, was there, and we wanted to find a way to honor her role in what was about to unfold for the nation. She loved Barney while he existed inside the friendly confines of our television screen but not so much when she ended up on stage with the massive character hovering over her. Our son Wade, her big brother, being the astute and sensitive person he is, noticed Leora was becoming horrified. He went on stage and gently guided her off. Perhaps that was a sign to me that getting close to this magical character had its dangers. My head and my heart said otherwise.

You can imagine the sadness that fell over me, before the series had a chance to establish itself, when I received a call from Mitch Semel, v.p. of programming at PBS on Friday, May 29, 1992, telling me that the first thirty episodes of the series would be it. We would not be funded going forward. I was incredulous and crestfallen.

All the work, hopes, and dreams would be dashed in what I recall as being a short phone call.

If you are wondering why this was done just as the series debuted with little time to demonstrate its power and impact on the intended audience, you can only imagine my frustration.

I do not recall pressing my case about the unfairness and wrong headedness of the decision because I had nothing to answer with except indignity. I had a lot of respect for those who had been in the system for some time. Ms. Lawson had worked at both CPB and PBS, and Mitch Semel had worked for several companies and had the respect of the programming community. Who was I to question the mysterious ways of the new programming shop? They must know something I do not.

Their decision could not have been based on modest reviews by ill-suited critics or the whispers of other children's producers, much better connected, saying that this Barney property should be on and off the PBS schedule as quickly as possible. Could it?

I also thought back as to what I could have done to make a stronger case for the series.

Or maybe it was all genetics; the Allen-to-Hartford connection was too weak a backstory to hold up against the light of more established players who would be given the benefit of any doubt.

Or maybe the marketing intensity that was building for Barney might have given PBS cold feet as they pondered the judgmental gaze of Peg Charren and her watchdog group.

Whatever the reasons, Jennifer and Mitch kept them to themselves. And I was too dumbfounded to delve at that time.

I had to share this news with Sheryl. Unlike the magical call over a year ago, this was one I was very reluctant to make. As I suggested earlier, Sheryl had a much better reaction than I did. With her equanimity and calm confidence fully on display, she said we would be all right. Thinking back, I still have a hard time understanding how she was not defiant and angry in the face of this devastating news. The mother of Barney just had this unwavering confidence that the children would render a different verdict.

I set about to regain my composure in the following days, hoping that the series would reveal itself or that we could do something to reverse this unfair death sentence.

Programmers across the system put it in their schedules, unaware of the decision that had been made with no regard for what Barney would do to affect our children's schedule.

Be reminded that the other two series we were in this test phase with by no means set the world on fire. Their ratings were average or below.

I consulted the tracking service we all subscribed to for ratings to see what was happening around the country, and in one market after another, Barney's numbers were holding up well against established series adjacent to it in schedules or, in fact, doing better business than those programs.

Meantime programmers were starting to get calls from parents asking more about this series that had just begun to dominate the imaginations of their children. Programmers told me that frantic parents would tell them stories about how mesmerized their children were with Barney, and they wanted to know where they could see him live or buy a plush representation or how many times a day, they could see the program on that channel.

The mania was taking hold in the hearts and minds of a younger preschool set than PBS had ever fully served.

The rumblings of what was happening in markets across the country had yet to reach the PBS C-Suite in Alexandria, Virginia. They had handed down their verdict before our part of the trial phase began. A series with less devotion from its intended audience, say one that was not fast becoming a cultural touchpoint for the whole society, could never have engineered the reversal of fortune that we were about to.

Here is where my role became as essential as the "phone call." I took some bold, and perhaps rule-bending steps, to make our case that this prejudgment of Barney would not stand.

First, I stayed in touch with programmers from major markets where Barney ratings were most easily compiled by the Nielsen Company so that I could share that information with others in more remote places. In fairness, whether a market was metered or had significant access to data was almost beside the point. Calls and letters were streaming into stations everywhere, wanting to know why their child had been taken under by the powerful spell of this new purple character.

I decided to bring Barney, the character, to Connecticut in June 1992 ahead of the disappointing call from PBS and before the crucial PBS Annual Meeting in San Francisco later that month. The word was seeping out, with a little help from interested parties, shall we say, that PBS was not going to feed the frenzy that was emerging throughout the country. Try explaining that decision to moms and dads who just knew it would have the same dreadful consequence for their children as taking away their favorite toys or most cherished possession. It was unthinkable.

Here is where I bent the rules. We have a code in the system against host selling on children's programs. Yet I did have Barney in the CPTV studio with messages of kindness and love while I and a partner made the financial ask. It was rather close to host selling, I will admit. I know two wrongs do not make a right, but desperate measures were needed to ensure I had the strongest case going into that meeting. We raised $50,000 on a Saturday morning in June in Connecticut when we would normally make a tenth, or less, of that.

We had more of a story to tell. And now this passion, we were confident, could turn into real dollars for the entire PBS system.

That afternoon we had a pre-planned live Barney appearance at the Hartford Civic Center. He would perform a few songs and talk to the children. When we arrived, there were five levels of screaming children laced to the top from the lobby area. I knew I was the closest I would ever come to replicating Beatlemania for the toddler set.

It was pandemonium. It was an amazing thing to behold as the joy and the love were shaking a building whose roof had collapsed during the blizzard of 1978. I thought it was going to come off again. Children were everywhere, screaming and shouting with joy, as their new obsession was about to entertain.

I vividly recall a few older children there who must have been dragged in by their parents. They wanted to spoil the fun and the magic for others in the younger set by revealing that Bob West, Barney's voice, was in the crowd among them. Bob gave them a look as if to say "Okay, you found me, but whatever you do, don't ruin it for the younger kids." They went along.

We videotaped the event and sent it around to programmers across the country just to amplify their awareness that this, too, could be converted into a host of opportunities to excite parents and raise dollars in their communities. If this is what happens in Hartford, imagine when Barney comes to Philadelphia, San Francisco, or Chicago.

The programmers were now convinced that what we were seeing was a megahit that comes along perhaps once in a generation. They might not have understood it, might have thought it had less educational heft than some other offerings (though it stood up to that criticism too), but the excitement it generated was a PBS station's dream scenario.

I knew that the major markets had untoward influence on PBS because they paid the bills and had the most sophisticated players on their staffs.

Arriving at the PBS meeting later in June, there was no indication from PBS that they were ready to change their minds. I worked the meeting like any political operative would. I set up friends from markets to address the question squarely from a microphone. I remember John Felton, a respected old-timer from WPBT in Miami, stepping forward with his large and angular frame, leaning against the mic, and bellowing about wanting more episodes of this Barney series. Others followed suit. The case was being made, and my invisible hand just kept working the room out of the sight of the PBS decision-makers.

As the meeting came to an end, Jennifer Lawson said that she had heard from enough programmers about their desire for more episodes of Barney, and she would begin negotiations with CPTV when we both arrived home. The PBS appeals court overturned the new chief program executive for the first time in history and, to the best of my knowledge, until I left the station some seventeen years later, the only time.

Now Barney was free to make history of its own.

Chapter 33: A Dinosaur Survives Attempts at Extinction

The Eagles sang, "Everybody's talking about the new kid in town." Barney was the new kid in town but not generally welcome on the block. The signs that this invasive species was not part of the ecosystem were, at times, subtle and, at other times, overt. There is no need to cite chapter and verse the slights and indignities all of us suffered owing to our attachment to Barney. The best salve was somehow getting to the party, the invitation having arrived the day before, and walking away with every prize—the cake and the cherry on top.

At one point Barney had as many videos topping the children's charts as Disney. That fact caught the attention of Michael Eisner and Jeffrey Katzenberg, the two top Disney executives at the time, who personally made a pilgrimage to Texas to find out what it would take to purchase this upstart.

Or Arnold Schwarzenegger catching up to Dennis DeShazer in an elevator as he was pursuing a Barney movie deal in Hollywood, and when told why he was in town, Arnold blurted out, "That is a big deal."

It is hard to understate the success of Barney on every level. Just a few numbers will illustrate the point.

Early on it boosted the entire children's block on PBS by 33 percent. Its impact was felt on other established series, delivering new audiences to each. It promoted family viewing as a third of the audience for the series was eighteen to forty-nine years of age. And it delivered diverse audiences to PBS, ranking number one among Hispanic children and number two among African American children.

There has long been this narrative that the spoils of Barney represented a one-way street, going into the pockets of our for-profit partners who themselves deficit funded the series beyond the PBS/CPB commitment.

While I suggested that I could have driven a harder bargain in the negotiations, it is hard to make any measurement that suggests that the system's investment in the production, $4.3 million for the first two seasons, for instance, was not returned many times over in pledge dollars, ratings, and buzz throughout the white lightning period of Barney, which extended over many years and a few generations of young children.

In membership drives in the early years, it accounted for two-thirds of the revenue generated. For instance, in one drive, the children's block nationwide earned $6.2 million, and $4.2 million of that was raised by Barney alone.

Late-night hosts and their jokes propelled Barney into the lexicon of American culture. It was everywhere. I can understand why we were envied and despised in equal measure.

The one true exception to that was, as you might imagine, Fred Rogers.

As Bob Dylan went electric at the 1965 Newport Jazz Festival, shocking his folk music adherents, in many ways I look at Barney as Fred goes electric, with more music, color, and pace. Hidden within was a comparable guide for children needing emotional reassurance that this world would be welcoming and kind. It was so because Barney said so.

Yale University, just down the road from where I live in Connecticut, played an important role in the campaign to bring legitimacy to Barney. I realized early on that while trying to temper marketing overreach by our partners, we had to solidify the educational bona fides of Barney, or this assault would continue unabated. It might turn out to be our Armageddon despite the children clamoring for more of everything related to Barney.

I became aware that Drs. Dorothy and Jerome Singer, a husband-and-wife team who taught at Yale and codirected the Yale University Family Television Research and Consultation Center, were big fans of Fred Rogers. In their research they were able to document his ability to make emotional connections in a simple, direct approach, with material purposefully directed at his audience. They had reservations about the vignette approach taken by *Sesame Street*.

I was introduced to the Singers by Laura Lee Simon, founder of the Connecticut Commission on Children, the state's leading child advocate, and a member of our board at CPTV. A more faithful servant to our state's children there never was. I was told that they saw many of the attributes they most liked in Fred Rogers in Barney and wanted to do more research to determine what their instincts told them was so age appropriate. I saw great value in encouraging this because of their reputation and the weight of the institution they represented.

My partners in Texas agreed to commission a study of season one, giving the Singers whatever they needed to examine the educational underpinnings of the series.

Let me stop here. Yes, the Texas producers funded the research, but there was no ability to have any say in the construct of their methodology or any way to influence their findings. I felt we needed some third-party validation as I was certain the rumblings within PBS were that success was all well and good but that they questioned whether the series could be justified in terms of educational value.

The Singers set about their work and came back with findings. Key among them was that there were over one hundred learning moments in each episode.

While those who did not want us to succeed felt that such scrutiny would be our kryptonite, it turned out to be our miracle cure for what might have otherwise proven to be a fatal disease. Instead, in the Singers' words, Barney was "almost a model of what a children's program should be." Phew!

As a result of this association, I ended up on a panel on children's programming at Yale in the spring of 1993, set up by the Singers. The true star on the panel was none other than Fred Rogers. Being in a room with him brings with it a sense that virtue and comfort have walked arm in arm into the building.

Before being on this panel with Fred, I heard him speak at a PBS Annual Meeting. I recall being able to hear a pin drop when he stood at the lectern. We hung on every word as each was so carefully chosen. After his talk, he stayed to greet each person in his patient and attentive way. Carmelita was attending this meeting and wanted to be sure to meet Fred. When she got to the head of the line, she was tearful in seconds as his gaze fell upon her. His aura was genuine and charismatic.

After reaching out to him to indicate what a privilege it was to present alongside him, his handwritten letter, dated April 7, 1993, arrived. It is a keepsake I cherish and keep in my office. It reads,

Just as I was about to write to thank you for being with us last week at Yale, your gracious letter arrived. Thank you for it and for helping with the Battell Chapel presentation. I would so much like to see and hear the tape which Barney made for the occasion. That was such a thoughtful gesture on all of your parts. I wish everybody could have seen and heard it well. I was singularly impressed by what you said. It's the motive that counts. You're so right. And thank you for your generous contribution to that evening. May you and Connecticut Public Broadcasting prosper and offer your best to your cities for many years to come.

Fred Rogers

Fred was an exceptional man in so many ways. His singular kindness to Barney and me in that moment was emblematic of a man who, I believe, recognized that what we were doing was validating the work he had been doing for children for so many years. There are many worse things than being wingman to Fred Rogers.

The overwhelming, never imagined success was something that various elements of the PBS family fully embraced while others remained at arm's length.

The programmers at local PBS stations were big fans. They loved the ratings and the pledge results. The general managers of those stations were fans because it was rare to have a series that had the whole community abuzz. Even if they took some ribbing from adults averse to the characteristics of Barney, which they found off-putting, the point was they knew it was a wild success and that station was credited with having it in its schedule.

Jim Scalem was a huge fan and gave us the honor of producing what I recall was the first national pledge event ever for a children's series.

Our partners were always accommodating when it came to special requests from us to serve the needs of stations with promos and visits by Barney to key markets involving the local stations.

We knew that our support came from the grassroots and not from the top. Though I will say that a smile crossed my face when I saw on a website, The HistoryMakers, that Jennifer Lawson's biography includes this sentence: "Lawson also developed children's series, "Barney and Friends," "Lamb Chop's Play-Along," and "Where in the World is Carmen Sandiego?"

In hindsight that is true. Now you know the rest of the story.

I like to say that nothing succeeds in America like excess. What was going on in the broad culture around this character was outrageous. People throughout the country were looking to capitalize on the craze with their fake, often putrid Barney costumes, entertaining at homes across the country, selling items that were not licensed by our partners, and trying to cash in in any way they could. I attribute much of the misgivings about us to what others did in our name. Who could control their urge to piggyback on something that had such appeal? It is my belief that an entire new channel, Nick Jr., developed in response to the market hole Barney was able to fill.

And while the merchandise was one thing, the real holy grail was trying to develop a character like Barney that could have the same appeal. If you notice, Nickelodeon had great success with *Blue's Clues* and *Dora the Explorer*, but development efforts surrounding a live action equivalent to Barney never materialized.

What my partners built, and we helped shape, was a once-in-a-generation phenomenon that defied gravity and much derision to arrive at a pantheon unattainable except to a handful of programs in history.

I was blessed to be a part of the ride.

Chapter 34: Sam's No Longer with Us

I may not have taken that ride were it not for the story of Sam Marantz. He was the founder of WXEL, the West Palm Beach, Florida, public television station, in 1982.

While I was mounting the campaign to save Barney at the PBS Annual Meeting, he was tucked away in a room at the conference hotel, interviewing candidates for general manager of that station. Evidently the general manager at the time was in hot water, and my father-in-law, John Viega Sr., a snowbird in the community, kept me apprised of what he saw in the local newspapers about the management's travails.

Sam had posted a notice on a board at the meeting saying that he was at the hotel and would meet with anyone interested in discussing an opening to head the station. I was too preoccupied to even read the notice, but a friend from CPTV, Mike Watt, who was at the meeting, later told me he had interviewed for the position. It intrigued me because it would be my opportunity to manage the entire operation in an attractive market, even though it was in the shadow of WPBT in Miami. My in-laws were already there a good portion of the year, and my mother would have moved with us despite her health issues. I told my colleague that I would like to contact Sam and made certain he was all right with that. He was.

Sam told me he would be going to Upstate New York to his daughter's place and that perhaps, given my location, I could meet him there. I took the long trip to Binghamton and stopped for a bite before I got there. All I could find in this barren area was a greasy hamburger joint. The food did not sit well with me. The place where Sam and I were to meet was closed in the winter, and having just reopened for the season, it wreaked of that stale, damp, musty feel. The combination of the greasy burger and the stale interior did me no good.

Despite that, he determined I was the right guy for the job. Do not ask me how. I felt I was making no sense throughout the interview, focused much more on my innards than my responses.

He laid out a timeline as to how this was all going to go down, and every phone conversation we had proved him to be a man of his word.

I recall coming back from a meeting on Barney in Dallas, connecting to Hartford through the just opened Pittsburgh International Airport, and thinking how strange it was that I had not heard from Sam based on the sequence he put forward. A few days later, I called him and let the call go to his message machine, which by now had a message recorded by a woman relaying the fact that "Sam is no longer with us." He had died in the interim. His wishes had never been conveyed to the board, and they began a new search process, one based on equal employment opportunity guidelines and not the whim of their founder. I knew that this would not work in my favor and passed on applying.

I think about all that I would have missed out on in the many years forward with Barney and other opportunities, which I will describe shortly.

Perhaps I imagined that bringing Barney to the system and saving its place for a whole generation of children, whose commitment and devotion would take it from there, was enough. As I think back, my stewardship for another seventeen years was more appreciated than I imagined.

The Lyons Group became Lyrick Studios over time and added new players, but two of the creators stayed on. For the last several years, of the original partners, only Dennis DeShazer remained. They also added a great new property, *Wishbone*, to their roster, under a separate creative team within the company.

While they resisted Disney's offer in the early days, in 2001, they agreed to sell Barney to HIT Entertainment. HIT is a British-American entertainment distribution company established in 1983, and it was the original international distribution arm of Jim Henson Productions. Previously it had been called Henson International Television, later reincorporated as HIT Communications PLC. After Jim Henson died, the business was sold to several members of the company's management, led by Peter Orton. They engineered a name change to HIT Entertainment to avoid any confusion and set its new path.

The two principals who were put in charge to guide Barney's future were Rob Lawes and Charlie Caminada. It is important to point out that there was no requirement that HIT Entertainment retain CPTV as a partner in the Barney production. Our most essential work was now to maintain what was well established.

Rob and Charlie did not retain us simply as an act of kindness; they truly respected what we had done and proved it by giving us the responsibility to manage the return to PBS of *Thomas the Tank Engine* in its original form, bringing the beautifully crafted animated series *Angelina Ballerina* to American shores, and moving *Bob the Builder* from Nickelodeon to PBS.

For this moment in time, CPTV was representing a group of wonderful children's properties and playing a vital role in carefully managing their place in the public television world. It was a joy to have been given these added responsibilities and revenue to add to our portfolio.

The period from 2001 on was a major turning point in my time at CPTV as I pared away most of my local responsibilities to focus on national programs, primarily in the areas of children's do-it-yourself series and in pledge specials.

It was a sad moment when Apax Partners, a venture capital group, bought these HIT Entertainment properties in 2005 and later decided to end our relationship in 2008.

Venture capital groups have one key consideration in mind—how do we squeeze more money out of whatever it is we have purchased?

There are generally two ways to do that. One is to cut expenses, and the other is to enhance revenues. Better yet, they usually proceed to mount a two-front attack on the bottom line from both directions. We were a casualty of that common play. They also took their properties and went to New York titan WNET, which was able to invest in the future production of episodes of *Angelina Ballerina*.

Although as a station we made many millions on Barney, those monies were readily converted into annual operating needs given our hand to mouth financial situation at the time.

Even the college fund obliquely promised to Leora went by the wayside.

Looking back on all this, I recognize that I owe Barney a lot more than it owes me. While I do not want my career defined by this one signature achievement, I could move on with a confidence I may never have had otherwise. It will be in the first paragraph of my obituary. The way I look at it, something that gave millions of children the sense that they were worthy and loved landing near the top of your list of how you are recalled is all right with me.

As a postscript to my Barney story, Mattel bought the property in 2011 from Apax and is said to be preparing to produce a movie. This revival is the brainchild of Academy Award–winning actor Daniel Kaluuya, a star of *Get Out* and *Judas and the Black Messiah*. It will be a live-action movie.

He has been quoted saying, "Barney was a ubiquitous figure in many of our childhoods, then he disappeared into the shadows, left misunderstood. We're excited to explore this compelling modern-day hero and see if his message of 'I love you, you love me' can stand the test of time." Barney's message in these fractious times will certainly have to cut through a lot of noise. Then again we had a trail of naysayers and doubters at our heels throughout.

Fred Rogers led the way with remarkable tributes in 2019, including documentaries and a film featuring Tom Hanks. Speaking for all those involved in the beginning, I can only hope for the same from this production group. Please play fair with the simplicity and beauty of what Barney meant to the adult millennials who will no doubt be attracted to the movie and bring their children with them.

Neil Genzlinger of the *New York Times* was one of the few who feted Barney on the twenty-fifth anniversary of its debut on PBS in 1992. The headline in his article, dated April 7, 2017, read, "The Blame for 'Barney'? I'm a Little Guilty." He also made certain Barney had its place in the *New York Times* piece dated October 13, 2020, titled, "Why We Turned to PBS: 50 Reasons Over 50 Years." Barney was number eighteen on the list.

In the 2017 piece, he described his inability to recall why Leora invited his daughter, the then four-year-old Emily, to our house to watch an episode of Barney. Neither can I. He does recall her staying a long time at our house, and I am sure it was because she, like millions of children who would follow, was mesmerized by that character and his gentle messaging.

He interviewed Leora, then thirty, to determine how she looked back at the whole experience. She admitted to him, "Especially when I was growing up, like when I went to high school, it wouldn't be a cool thing to talk about." With the passage of time, and a master's degree from the University of Pennsylvania in, what else, positive psychology, she and Barney have come together once again, sharing a desire to look at the world in a hopeful way.

Positive psychology is not sunshine and lollipops, I have come to learn. Does all psychology have to be focused on aberrant behavior? Recognizing that the love for others begins with the long and complicated process of loving yourself is a good jumping-off point. Perhaps if we focus on what's right with people and encourage more of that behavior in all of us, we might make this place a bit kinder.

Not too bad a message to start off life with, wouldn't you say?

Chapter 35: Bigger Than Barney

To start a child's life with a positive message about hope and possibility is a wonderful use of the medium of television.

So, too, is hearing from an indigent man in Hartford who, had it not been for public television and its nature programs, may never have learned so much about the animals of the wild kingdom. He was so grateful for the exposure he gained to continents he will never personally explore.

He is certainly not the person most people imagine as the public television "demographic." We love to pigeonhole people by virtue of their background, ethnicity, status, or wealth and project expectations that this is who they are, what they believe, and what type of entertainment or information they must consume.

The Hartford man's story is more common than one might imagine. Were it not for public television, enrichment of all sorts, including the arts, culture, and history, would be absent in the lives of so many Americans.

As a programmer, you look for ways to meet unmet needs in your community. That concept is amorphous, I grant you, but I was blessed to see it literally come to life. It occurred in such a profound way that I would have to say the next reveal in this book had more impact on our station and our state than even the uproar and impact of Barney. That might be difficult to believe given the story of Barney.

What happened in 1994, just a scant two years after Barney's debut, was stunning.

Still riding high on this megahit, my focus was bifurcated. Despite running the national programming shop, Connecticut-based programming remained my first love. Given my great staff, I was able to stay astride both in this seminal year of 1994 when we would win more Boston/New England Emmy Awards than any of the Boston stations, a first in history, and bring to our audience a new local programming champion.

A state representative, Fred Gelsi, approached Jerry Franklin about the excitement developing around the University of Connecticut women's basketball team. While they had not won a national title at that point, they had been to a Final Four and were led by a dynamic coach, Geno Auriemma. They had recruited some great players to accomplish his mission of a national championship.

Representative Gelsi asked if we had ever considered airing any of their games. Jerry said that it was not really on our radar, but he would discuss it with me.

When he first mentioned the possibility, just one name entered my mind—Rebecca Lobo. I thought that her name was something out of the Wild West. In strides, L-O-B-O. Could a programming decision this momentous be built on the framework of one name? Perhaps.

We had all seen her and others in one-minute highlight packages on the eleven o'clock news, but that was it. Except for those who went out of their way to get to Storrs, Connecticut, the home of my alma mater, they were seldom seen by most Connecticut residents.

We were told by UConn officials that there would be production in place for the final game of the Big East tournament and a few games in the NCAA tournament that followed. Therefore, little money would be needed to acquire the rights. In truth, no one else in our market had an interest.

I really had to pause on this one since we were in the middle of our major on-air fundraising event of the year—what was then called the March Festival. However, that name, that dominant presence of Rebecca Lobo, kept coming to mind.

How could testing a few games really affect our fundraising or upset the public television "demographic"? There, I said it again. I never had a self-limiting view of our audience. Perhaps that came from my hybrid instincts, juxtaposing a commercial engine in a public television chassis. I said, "Let's try it."

I often wonder whether Jerry Franklin would have overruled me had I balked. Given that Fred Gelsi had a lot to do with our capital budget funding from the state of Connecticut, he might have in order not to jeopardize the support. I believe he would have done it with hesitancy. By this point he had really begun to trust my instincts and let me run my own shop.

Mind you, at that moment I was not making a long-term programming decision that would dominate the next eighteen years of our existence. It was one game at a time with the few that were available to us until CBS nationally came in to swoop up the Final Four, should UConn get that far.

I would go out in front of our audience personally to receive the verdict. Did we make the right decision?

That is the great thing about public television. You need no middleman, no rating service, no higher authority to tell you whether you have met an unmet need. You can go right to the source. The phones started ringing that first magical night, and they never stopped until we aired our last game in 2011.

I was somewhat surprised by the response that first night. We had little promotion surrounding the broadcast, sports were not common to our service, and women playing basketball then was not the cultural touchpoint it has become.

CPTV had a history of occasional forays into sports programming, including Aetna World Cup tennis, Ivy League football, and curling. Yes, curling.

Is it fair to surmise that there were regular viewers not happy with the decision? Certainly there were the detractors, and they let us know. Their concerns were drowned out for that one night by the cacophony of phones ringing off the hook in studio.

I noticed an interesting thing as we asked for support during the game. When we went into a break on the heels of a great shot or heroic act by UConn, the phones lit up. If, however, we went into the break with the opposing team scoring on UConn, the response was tepid. That tendency would reoccur throughout our time as their broadcast partner. What was amazing, in hindsight, was how infrequently UConn fell behind in any game in all those years.

There is an adage that the best way to kill a bad product is to advertise it. Geno gave us a great product from start to finish, and the relationship we built was unparalleled in the history of public television. In fact, by any measure, this was the most successful long-term local franchise in the history of public television. That is if you measure it by ratings, membership dollars, sponsorships, and impact on the fortunes of a local station.

UConn women's basketball became our defining and indispensable characteristic to people who previously never watched public television. It also became the greatest promotional tool in our arsenal. A promotional message for another program in the context of a game, given the astounding ratings, tying one end of the state to another, was something we otherwise could never have afforded if it were paid media. And how about the people who fell asleep during UConn blowout after UConn blowout and woke up to a concert or documentary that they otherwise would never have watched?

UConn women's basketball took CPTV from a boutique, appreciated service to Connecticut's version of must-see TV. It gave us a live quality of appointment viewing that we never imagined possible.

That first night we might have made history for public television; when taking the broadcast feed, we did not clip a full-out thirty-second Ford commercial. There it was, and the world survived. One might say it was the precursor to "enhanced underwriting" as it would later be called.

We decided to continue into the NCAA tournament in 1994 to see whether the one-night phenomenon was indeed something to build on. As I recall, we did well again, but I had a family vacation planned to visit my in-laws in Florida and left after that second game.

I called back to the station to find that we were unable to get $5,000 in underwriting to cover basic costs of the next game, and back at the station, talk was of not doing any more games. I told Lisa that I had to talk to Jerry about this. I convinced him that no matter what, we had to ride this season to the very end. It was a hunch I had.

When our ride ended, it would be a decision that someone else made—not our own.

We had to prove to UConn that the public television station could be a reliable partner, even with so little experience in live sports programming. So thankfully I prevailed and thus set up the opportunity in front of us for 1995, which happened to coincide with the first undefeated championship season in UConn women's basketball history.

Chapter 36: 35-0

I was in meetings in New York City on January 15, 1998. It was a typical winter day in the Northeast with intermittent snow and icy conditions. I had to get back home because it was our twentieth wedding anniversary.

I was coming back from the New Haven train station through Cheshire, a town adjacent to my own. I was stopped in a procession of cars going slowly on a flat surface. Fearing black ice, an older gentleman slid perilously close to my car and just touched it. While he got out of his car, another person plowed into his vehicle. That's the way these daisy chains work.

As we all got out to assess whether there was damage, he recognized me as "that guy on television" and proceeded to try to sell me on showcasing his barbershop quartet. I was not my best self at that moment and curtly told him, "Yes, I am that guy, but right now I'm the guy whose bumper it looks like you tapped and who is due home to celebrate a milestone with my wife."

UConn women's basketball made me a household figure in the state. While I had been fundraising on air for years prior, this franchise changed everything. UConn had given me a Starter jacket with their logo on it to pledge the first game. It ended up in their Hall of Fame on campus, replaced by one I never liked as much but still possess.

Jerry Franklin, Harriet Unger, our basketball executive producer, and I were feted at a UConn game years later at the Hartford Civic Center, joining UConn officials at center court awash in the adoration of rabid UConn fans. This is not the stuff that most programming executives ever feel from an audience. At best we can sense their appreciation in numbers, not in wild applause.

To understand this phenomenon, we need to go back to 1995.

After stumbling upon something special in 1994, the question was, what would we do in 1995?

UConn Athletics was headed by Lew Perkins, a larger-than-life figure. He was shrewd and calculating, sometimes gruff, sometimes charming, but saw that his athletic department was really built on the back of what legendary coach Jim Calhoun had done with men's basketball.

He took pride in what women's basketball head coach Geno Auriemma was doing. I am not certain that even he felt women's basketball, while the highest profile of the women's sports required by a university under Title IX equity provisions, was ever going to be a moneymaker. To each party its value was unknown.

In 1995 there was no attempt to formalize the relationship through a contract, just a handshake agreement to afford CPTV the opportunity to do as many games as we could afford. In that year production was not in place in all places, so we would have to bear the cost exclusively.

This was all new to us. UConn suggested people who might be interested in supporting this fledging effort. We hired a man by the name of Paul Karlsson, who did much of the East Coast business setting up remote production facilities throughout the college sports world. He was a great guide to negotiating rates and remote trucks and helping us to staff it as our crew was not large or experienced enough to take it on.

UConn had a great relationship with sports producer Terri Schindler,

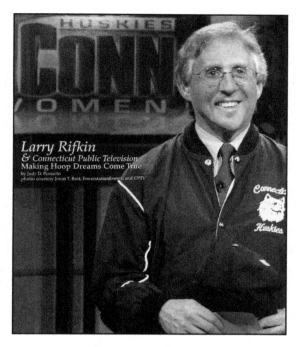

*Larry on-air during a
UConn women's basketball game*

a woman who could easily make our games look professional. It did not hurt that her husband, Mike Gorman, longtime Celtics play-by-play man, was coaxed by his wife to come along for this experiment.

Therefore our games had a patina of professionalism from the start.

We agreed to do eleven games that year, and the bonanza of support continued unabated. Some games were picked up by national services, among them ESPN and CBS. These were the marquee value matchups, for example, with archrival Tennessee. Most of the games available to us were with Big East teams that UConn decisively outclassed.

It really did not matter to our audience. The margin of victory had little bearing on the growing groundswell of support and love for this team.

Not only did Geno Auriemma and associate head coach Chris Dailey select great players, but they also selected fine young women who were great representatives of the university.

Born in Italy, Geno had that immigrant attitude that he had ground to make up in America. Diminutive in size yet driven by that inexplicable thing only certain people have inside, he is one of the most gifted motivators and psychologists I have ever met. He has this gift of bringing a player down to build her back up. As tough as he can be, only a handful of young women have transferred out of his program. Given the rigor of his practices and demands for excellence, you might have expected more to exodus. He is a highly sought-after speaker in Connecticut and elsewhere. He is a charming, disarming presence when interviewed on national television.

I recall a banquet honoring one of the countless national championship teams he led to victory where he introduced each of his players in his "break 'em down to build 'em up" style. In his introduction of a slow-footed center, he started off by saying that she could not jump over the Hartford phone book. However, he then went on to tell you that the screens she set were bone crunching, and she had the heart of a champion.

At a reception at the station one year with 150 people crowded into our studio to spend time with the athletes, Geno stepped up to the mic to regale people with his laser-like assessment of all things UConn. I introduced him, and he stepped forward to very loud applause. His assessment was caustic and truly his own. "I didn't hear the players clapping very loud," he opined. As he described the great Swin Cash, his take was uniquely his. "Swin's perfect. Except when she dribbles or shoots or passes."

A serious premed student on the team got his treatment of what her bedside manner will be like. "She's not as weird as she used to be…She comes by the office and says hi. Last week I saw her teeth for the first time." What a character, Geno is.

John Walters, a longtime *Sports Illustrated* reporter, published a book in 2002 titled *The Same River Twice: A Season with Geno Auriemma and the Connecticut Huskies*. In it he writes, "Larry Rifkin is a visionary. So is Geno Auriemma." While I am flattered to be mentioned anywhere alongside this legendary, now Hall of Fame, coach, among the greatest ever to direct a major college or pro sports team in my favorite sport, the comparison is wildly off target. Geno's brilliance, longevity, and passion put him into a category far beyond my reach.

But as Geno said about CPTV at Jerry Franklin's farewell event in 2019, "What good is being great if nobody knows about it, and that's what CPTV accomplished for us." That was another astute observation.

UConn women's basketball, relegated to snippets on the eleven o'clock news, long might have excelled in the quiet confines of Gampel Pavilion had we not come along. But as we went on, they became the women's college basketball team with the best television contract in the nation, and we became the envy of public television stations in the country.

Isn't that the best type of business relationship? One that works for both parties. I should have written *Art of the Deal*. Of course, now we know Tony Schwartz, not Donald Trump, did that.

Geno was celebrated throughout the land, welcomed into the homes of recruits on their radar, with a big plus in his back pocket. Virtually every game you play in will be seen statewide, if not nationally. Even the vaunted Pat Summitt could not offer that.

And CPTV was pulling down ratings, game after game, that approached—and often exceeded—double digits, with averages of eight or nine (nearly 150,000 viewers in our dominant market area). The ratings could go as high as a fourteen or fifteen. This was unheard of! Perhaps Ken Burns's classic documentary series *The Civil War* would do gangbusters business of a five or a six as a limited series, but consistent numbers nearing ten? It defied all laws of public television gravity.

My programming colleagues around the nation received analysis of ratings from PMN Trac, a public television service run by Drs. Judith and David LeRoy, and the top three programs in any given week during the season would be UConn women's basketball. It was unlike anything other stations anywhere had experienced before or since.

The most popular game each year was senior night when we would capture teary send-offs for all the young women we adored for the past four years. The phone calls were an avalanche. I assure you that the ability to raise $100,000 in one night was not normal. Yet with UConn Senior Night, it was possible.

The continuity aspect of women's basketball set it apart from the men's team. The players stayed all four years and built a base of loyalty unavailable to the men's team, where the best players would be plucked from the team in their sophomore or junior year to go to a professional league.

Television is a character-driven medium. With UConn women's basketball, we had that. And, of course, the importance of having coaches out of central casting who never left didn't hurt either.

Now back in 1995, our first season of coverage, the team was awesome. It went 35–0.

It was Rebecca Lobo's farewell season and had the makings of perfect drama night in and night out as we chased the towering achievements of the University of Tennessee program. UConn was still the underdog at this stage. We set up a "good guys versus bad guys" scenario between the two teams. UConn battled its way to number one in the nation when it toppled Tennessee on a nationally televised Martin Luther King Jr. Day showdown. Like the classic UCLA-Houston men's basketball game some years earlier, this was a coming-of-age moment for women's college basketball.

When UConn hoisted the trophy as national champions for the first time that year, we rode that achievement to a prominent position in the season-ending celebratory parade in the canyons of downtown Hartford.

We were officially beloved for taking a chance on airing women's basketball. I can still hear cries of "We love you, CPTV!" and finger-pointing saying, "Yes, you did it!"

It is important to understand that UConn women's basketball in Connecticut is loved by people who hate sports. Really. It is particularly noteworthy that the team is beloved by older women. You will see in the first few paragraphs of obituaries throughout the state's newspapers something like this: "And she never missed a UConn women's basketball game on television." Appointment books and calendars were marked to indicate that in that two-hour period on game day, nothing else mattered. Do not call! Such a madness was the stuff of fantasies for a television station. We were told of a woman who, when police arrived for a wellness check, refused to answer her door until the game concluded.

We started to learn how to capitalize on the delirium by doing special shows with Geno Auriemma, interviews, and call-ins using his personality and celebrity and not letting a season end until we had captured it all in heartrending documentary as we did in 1995 called, you guessed it, *35–0*.

By the end of 1995, Lew Perkins and UConn clearly knew they had something of value here. It was something we would have to negotiate to keep.

I had to wonder whether we could hold on to this station-redefining powerhouse.

Chapter 37: Let's Roll the Dice

The decision to experiment with UConn women's basketball was one thing as it required little risk, but keeping it there was really the more difficult challenge. Now that its value was known, the stakes were much higher.

I alluded to the decision on March 7, 1994, to take the journey in the Big East tournament and carry the final against Seton Hall, a game UConn won 77–51, a precursor of many blowouts to come. It was then paramount that we follow the team through the NCAA tournament to its conclusion. I think that was the first critical decision in ensuring a chance to make this relationship long term.

I saw Lew Perkins as a person who would not forget slights, real or imagined. He saw himself as principled and expected a certain respect from partners.

In 1996 we faced another crucial decision. Jerry Franklin had an inkling that Lew Perkins wanted a split presence on commercial and public television in Connecticut. He wanted us to share the franchise with a more established commercial station. He set me about the task of visiting with the commercial stations in the state to see what kind of shared arrangement we might negotiate. I did my due diligence, and with two weeks to go in a formal request for proposal process set up by the school, conforming to state guidelines, I went to Jerry and said that after much consideration, it was my firm belief that we go it alone. He pressed me, of course, as he should. It was perhaps the most momentous decision in the station's history.

I will put forward the bold assertion that no decision was as transformative as this one on the fortunes of any local television station—ever! This may sound like hyperbole, but I cannot imagine one that affected every aspect of the company, in as positive and sustained ways.

With Barney, while a few people in the building touched it, the programming department basked in the glory. Donna Collins, our sales manager, who had a commercial background, stepped forward and obtained Huggies's support as a national underwriter. Patrice Pascual, Anita Ford Saunders, and Lee Newton took on promotional responsibilities for the series over different spans of time. Heather Kelsey kept an accounting of the involved finances, Paul Pfeffer produced a stream of new promos for stations, Marcie Wnuk made certain new Barney product was available to stations, and Scott Phillips provided valuable marketing information throughout much of the time. Beyond that Lisa and I were the constants in the Barney project from day one.

UConn women's basketball touched everyone on staff in some way. The production and engineering staff worked the games and enhanced their skills. The promotion department had a story to tell that was historic for the station. The underwriting and membership departments designed packages and opportunities to capitalize on this juggernaut. Board members swelled with pride as their colleagues congratulated them on this stroke of genius.

At this critical juncture, if I was correct, we would win big time. If I was wrong, we would second-guess the decision for a long time. My reasoning was this. While the commercial stations were beholden to their networks to run the national programming, they might only be able to broadcast a limited number of games. However, given their overall audiences and promotional capabilities, even if they aired three games and we aired fifteen in a season, the perception of those numbers was likely to be reversed in the public's mind because of the bullhorn of local news that they would use to ballyhoo their involvement. Thus, the impact would be to diminish the value of the franchise as a membership vehicle, which was key in my mind. I could hear a viewer saying, "Why should I give to CPTV when I can get some of the games elsewhere?"

A diluted, shared arrangement would have limited the unparalleled impact of the franchise in the ways that I have mentioned and more that are less direct. For example, many members of the state legislature are UConn graduates. Our relationship with UConn had a salubrious effect on any ask we might make in those chambers.

To Jerry's great credit, despite what he thought Lew Perkins wanted, he agreed with me, and so we rolled the dice. We sweetened the offer with much special programming, including an athletic director's show, the *Geno Auriemma Show*, year-ending specials and just about anything we could imagine they would want. We even took on the sad sister, UConn Football, mired in the Yankee Conference as I discussed earlier.

While I thought the commercial stations could not come forward with the volume of content we were offering, I really did not know what would result. Could two commercial partners ever come together? Could an emerging regional sports network partner with a local commercial station blow our proposal out of the water? In truth, none of that happened, and we won the contract after some involved negotiations with Lew Perkins and his associate athletic director, Jeff Hathaway, who would later take his position when Lew moved on to the University of Kansas.

Here was the deal: three years, $2.28 million in June 1995, which included fifty-one games and three road football games. Our bid carried a price tag of $8,000 for the rights to each game, which was lower than the commercial stations, but as I suspected, the total number of games we could guarantee sealed the deal. The CBS affiliate proposed to air ten games at $15,000 apiece, while the NBC affiliate offered three games at $10,000 apiece. We won it outright and negotiated a series of extensions along the eighteen-year road paved with gold for both parties.

It was never an easy contract to manage with the many secret handshakes of college athletics and unreadable provisions in their NCAA rule books, new to us, but it was so worth it. Over time it became wash, rinse, and repeat.

With great teams each year, quality players rotating through, and Geno's overwhelming personality and presence a constant, CPTV rung every ounce of value we could out of the relationship.

Remember my reference to how well our on-air fundraising went when UConn was leading in a game? Imagine this, at a point when I stopped counting, though I think it was 2002, seven full years into our relationship, UConn had won 124 games on our air and lost just two over that span!

Marquee matchups, games likely to be competitive, were negotiated away to national networks by the Big East and NCAA. ESPN is located in Bristol, Connecticut. To be sure, its rise and success is a remarkable media story. Just as Nickelodeon watched our Barney success with great longing, ESPN programmers would watch UConn games on our air, imagining that it might be possible to replicate that success across the nation. They saw our capacity crowds, frenzied fans, and a great product on the court and considered replicating it on a national level.

We had reason throughout our years as UConn's broadcast partner to work with ESPN, and they told us how much our experiment impressed them. We even aired a UConn men's game, produced by ESPN, because of a scheduling snafu.

In the course of our "first and best in the nation women's basketball package," ESPN bought the entire Big East and NCAA women's basketball tournaments, and the WNBA was born. The WNBA had the makings of the next step league for all the stars UConn was producing.

You can call it coincidence, but I think there is a case to be made that children's television and women's sports piggybacked on what we started.

Over the years I turned much of the management of the UConn project over to Harriet Unger, who I mentioned before in these pages. The job she did in attending to every detail surrounding the program was remarkable. She organized and coordinated the many game details involved, produced and directed the interview programs attached to the games, and even produced a preseason special, traveling with the team to Europe one season to document their trip. She became a favorite of team members.

While small in stature, as indicated by her current production company, Short Girl Productions, she is whip smart and tireless in making television programming of all kinds perform to its capacity. And given that her background was in fundraising when she first arrived at the station, she always knew how to maximize a production for its full effect on the bottom line.

In an article in the *Hartford Courant*, Connecticut's most celebrated sports columnist, Jeff Jacobs, came to the station to watch us "pledge" a game. In the article titled "Mr. Rifkin's Neighborhood," dated March 5, 2001, he said, "New York has the World's Most Famous Arena and the center field monuments. Boston has a Green Monster and a parquet floor. Connecticut, well, Connecticut has the CPTV pledge break." In his breezy style, he went on to say, "Seven years into one of the great experiments in the history of public television, I am prepared to pay homage to the grand wizard of state sports TV." And my response to him was "Slow news days, eh?" His reply was that "this is *the* place".

And in hindsight it was for this remarkable moment in time.

While I usually kept my head down, perhaps to avoid all the incoming on Barney, I must say on this one, I held my head up and proudly represented the project for seventeen years on our air.

I pledged the first game and was there to say goodbye in 2011, when UConn decided to seek greener pastures on SNY in New York. And each night throughout, I took great care in crafting a message to reach the audience. I worked tirelessly to freshen some time-worn concepts about our commitment, our dedication, and the substantial cost in providing these games. We promised our audience that we would broadcast every game available to us, traveling across the country and even to Puerto Rico to produce the Caribbean Classic tournament that was held in a hotel's ballroom.

I imagined it was the same audience tuning in to each game, so I had to find new ways into their hearts. Oh, I had my chestnuts like, "CPTV was there before all the shouting really started, before the first banner was hung celebrating a national championship…We took the risk no one else would make, and we made the call for you!" I believed that message. And given their unflagging support through the years, those watching did too.

Chapter 38: Sixth Man Benched for Good

Years after I left CPTV, people would approach me and bemoan the fact that UConn women's basketball was no longer on the station.

Despite what you often hear about how pledge breaks annoy people, when it came to UConn, we were the "sixth man" for the women's team. We became a part of the whole experience, just as much as the players, the coaches, and our announcers. It was a package that people came to expect, a friend whose visit was always welcomed.

As it went along, our presence grew because with each new contract, we added more dollars, more games, high-definition broadcasts, and streaming, and thus we had to seek more support from fans to pay for these things.

I rarely went to a game in person because I was always in studio pledging the games.

The flagship station, the women's sports pioneer, was sidelined after televising over four hundred games in an eighteen-year stretch.

I took an early retirement from CPTV in spring 2009 but stayed on as a consultant on national programming into 2011 as the final round of

UConn negotiations was going on.

For whatever reason, Jerry Franklin did not invite me into the negotiating process. I was an integral part of every negotiation since the beginning, but there were new administrators at UConn, and perhaps Jerry felt he knew them better and could handle this round in a solo fashion. I am not saying that he miscalculated here by any means. I think the relationship had run its course because UConn's new president, Susan Herbst, lacked context in making the decision. Coming from out of state, she did not really appreciate the beauty and the symmetry of it all. She probably thought that the pledging was annoying and provincial. To the true UConn fan, it was not.

The state's flagship public university and its nonprofit statewide public television partner coming together in a harmonious marriage to seal the arrival of women's college sports as a true phenomenon demonstrated that this fan base was more rabid than its high-profile men's team.

My early justification for the preemption of great PBS programming in the heart of the winter, when more television is consumed than any other time of year, was that it transcended sports and was justifiable for the message it sent about gender equity and for the opportunity it provided to showcase the best of my alma mater's student base—the true college athlete.

In newspaper accounts, President Herbst said all the right things when she kicked CPTV to the curb despite the fact the numbers that CPTV put on the table were not dramatically different from those of SNY. She said, "CPTV has been a loyal and dedicated partner, and both CPTV and UConn have benefited from the relationship." Jerry Franklin said, "I just got up and got the UConn tread marks off my back." Good for Jerry, saying what needed to be said.

The one true justification for Herbst's action was that her teams had to find refuge in an inferior league, the American Athletic Conference, as the Big East reorganized without football schools. I am confident in saying that she saw UConn's presence in the New York market as her ace in the hole in trying to place UConn in a major Power 5 conference in the future. She needed that because of the serious, and perhaps misguided, resources poured into the school's football program.

While UConn has now returned to the Big East in 2020 and remains on SNY through an arrangement with ESPN, which owns the conference package, I will argue that the benching of the "sixth man" never accomplished what they intended.

I recall an article written by a Connecticut newspaper suggesting that UConn had outgrown CPTV. I had to respond. I wrote the reporter a letter telling him how off base I thought his observations were. They had won seven championships on our air, attained unobtainable winning streaks on several occasions, recruited great women and great players from as far away as Saint Petersburg—Russia, that is—and had all the national exposure of any college team in any sport while maintaining their local presence on our air. The only exception perhaps was Notre Dame football, which had its own national network at the time.

All the while attendance at home games stayed consistently high and in the top three in the nation.

In the seasons from 2005–2006 through 2011–2012, CPTV reached an average of fifty-six thousand households in the Hartford portion of the statewide viewing area alone. That roughly converted to eighty-four thousand people, and that does not capture viewing throughout the rest of the state and on CPTV's streaming platform. Some games, such as the victory over DePaul on January 28, 2006, saw a doubling of those numbers.

CPTV finally had a calling card beckoning people in Fairfield County and elsewhere who watched incoming PBS channels from New York and Boston. And now it was gone.

Geno Auriemma is a truth teller. At times he conveys hard truths to his players. While we see excellence on the court, he sees so much more and expects much greater results. "She shoots too much. She shoots too little." UConn held a team to fifty-seven points. Geno sees holes in the defense. He has a different looking glass than we do.

Over the course of our eighteen-year partnership, UConn was a combined 612–48 (.927) with seven national championships and twelve Final Four appearances.

He gave us excellence. We gave him a great television home. It was a perfect marriage.

Even the far-seeing Geno Auriemma admitted that he did not envision such a great impact on his program. He was quoted as saying, "At the time, I really didn't give it much thought because I didn't really think it was going to evolve into, 'Hey that's our NESN(New England Sports Network). That's our YES Network.' I had no idea. And then it turned out to be probably the greatest thing that's ever happened to our program and the greatest thing that's ever happened to them." There goes Geno telling the truth once again.

Chapter 39: Competing with Ghosts

It was September 11, 2001. I was at my home office for the first time. I had worked out an agreement with Jerry that I could work from home a few days of the week.

Nearly twenty years after arriving at CPTV for the ride of my life, I was becoming disenchanted with some of the mundane responsibilities. I did not want to attend countless, and often pointless, meetings and felt that I was growing apart from the institutional requirements of a department head.

I guess I felt I had earned the privilege of writing a new ticket. And while I would not say that my work there was done, I was beginning to compete with ghosts.

Grant you, Barney, UConn, and many other programming projects had me fully engaged, but I could sense I was becoming restless.

Even during the 1990s and into the 2000s, I would scoop up my family and visit radio stations in out-of-the-way New England hamlets. I still longed for that total immersion in a community as the broadcaster of record, the type I remembered my father being when I grew up. We would drive up the road to Great Barrington, Massachusetts, and listen to their local station, driving past it and back on beautiful Route 7.

I had a small dalliance with a station on the southern tip of Maine and flew up to discuss buying a station in Bar Harbor. As I studied their financials, I realized that these were great opportunities to go broke. With Bar Harbor, it was off-season most of the year. I found half the retail outlets in the area closed for the season. And there was no way that you could prove that visitors in the summer and fall were listening to the station.

My most serious inquiry involving a radio broker was considering the purchase at WFAD in Middlebury, Vermont. It was perhaps the most realistic opportunity of the group. Unfortunately, after numerous nice trips to the area and a look at their books, I realized that unless I became, in effect, a college station with an annual advertising and programming alliance with Middlebury College, it was pointless. I really did not want to own a college radio station. Vermont towns are very spread out. People seemed to shop in town and did not have much choice, so advertising was unnecessary.

The books they kept were so incomplete I had to go to a car dealer in town and ask the owner how much they spent with the station each year. He indicated it was $1,600. "You mean $16,000?" I asked again, incredulous at the number. "No," he replied, "$1,600."

Let me be clear. I love New England, and I love towns that are a bit in need of repair. Well, I do hail from Waterbury, Connecticut, after all. And I am a big fan of Richard Russo novels about these places and the people who hang in there, long after the days of wine and roses have passed. I love the bones of these places and the sense that maybe all of us fractured folks can put ourselves and our town back together.

However, the sanctuary of CPTV allowed me to dream, explore, and pursue and then plan a hasty retreat from what would have been almost certain disaster. It was a game I played with myself, knowing that any opportunity good enough to pursue, I couldn't afford. And the rest weren't worth taking.

The last one I pursued was probably the most obvious target—WATR in Waterbury. It was a north star in my hometown and the one that brought my dad and mom together and gave me my first television experience with the Easter Seals telethon; my first dalliance with a true broadcasting phenomenon on their FM, WWYZ; and a certain sense that I could always come home and be welcomed.

I asked to meet with Mark Gilmore, the owner most engaged with the operations of the station. It has now been in his family for eighty years. He brought along the station's general manager, Tom Chute, who has long been the morning personality in Waterbury.

He is well regarded for his talents as a morning host, director, and actor in regional theater and his time behind the mic singing standards in many performances in the area. He and I always got along well, but it was awkward discussing the purchase of the station when the natural order of things would suggest it first be made available to him to put a group together then buy the station. Quickly I turned from this subject to my interest in getting back behind a radio mic and doing talk radio.

WATR's format has been very eclectic in the modern day of the eclipse of local AM radio. There are talk, news, music, ethnic programs, sports talk—you name it.

We worked out an arrangement whereby I could get sponsors and do a Saturday program, which might scratch my itch in local, community radio without requiring me to leave CPTV or go broke in the process.

At the time I had no interest in doing any radio on CPTV's sister radio station, Connecticut Public Radio. Perhaps I just wanted to be more opinionated than much of the public affairs programming on public radio would allow. Or I wanted to keep my statewide persona a television-only proposition, and I wanted to start "off Broadway" to try out my own form of a program in a smaller, no-risk market. I also did not necessarily have confidence that I would easily find my voice in this format. I was never going to be a bombastic, carnival barker as big-time talk radio required.

I used to listen to the great New York talkers, such as Barry Gray, Barry Farber, and of course Bob Grant. Regardless of their politics, left or right, I was impressed by their style, confidence, and surety behind the mic. It was a great gift.

My political views, as mentioned, were moderate to left leaning, but I thought that there had to be a way to use this medium to good effect to entertain but truly inform and help organize the thinking of a community.

Bottom line, perhaps, I just wanted to go back home and see if that small-town dream was still something that attracted me. I had to be honest. I was never leaving Connecticut.

My radio ownership forays were wanderlust. I had been offered an opportunity at PBS at one point and turned it down, not wanting to be part of the bureaucracy. Enamored with the thought of moving to Southern California, I had sought an opportunity at KPBS in San Diego. I was offered the job at a salary commensurate with what I was making at CPTV. However, they could not guarantee that they would be able to cobble funding sources together to make it stick in year two.

So I stayed on "after the lovin'," to quote Engelbert Humperdinck. I was not totally disenchanted, just a step out of place, trying to find the next big thing. It would never come. The go-go days from the late 1980s to early 2000s could never be duplicated.

I stayed on and augmented my day job with this growing desire to prove myself on radio on weekends. In that way it was a full and rich time.

From a programming standpoint, many of the concerts and pledge specials I described in earlier chapters, such as *Ipi N'tombi*, and the management of the range of HIT properties that came our way in the wake of Barney were fulfilling.

And there were modest successes, such as aligning with a delightful man, Chris Cerf, Bennett Cerf's son and a founder of the Harvard Lampoon, now a children's programming producer, on a series called *Lomax, the*

Hound of Music. It was a wonderful project. But it was not Barney.

And there were misses, for sure. And some were painful. I was introduced to a children's producer in Connecticut, who by the time we met was led to believe that because I had made Barney a hit, I could preordain the success of his project if I signed on. No matter how often I reminded him that his project, on safety messaging for children, replete with an adorable lead character, was not Barney, he could never hear that admonition. His series needed much work, and I made him pay extravagantly for our involvement and help in conforming to public television standards. The price of entry for bringing us in as partners, as I recall, was about $200,000.

Money became a major consideration for my national programming unit. By this point Barney revenue and UConn revenue were baked into the station's budget. Ho hum, what now?

Mature properties are often taken for granted, no matter their size and import.

I recognized that I was beginning to get involved with outside producers and projects that I knew would be difficult to manage and that did not appeal to me. I had become a keen judge of the types of people and projects that would haunt me. The question was, would I be able to avoid taking them on if the dollars involved were too compelling to look away? I really did not want to begin making bad choices for financial reasons. I had worked too hard to maintain a level of integrity that was important to me.

I did not mind taking risks with great producers such as Aida Moreno of *Antiques Roadshow* fame, on ballroom dancing instructional program, another of her specialties, or Tatge-Lasseur on *Breaking the Silence: Children's Stories*, focusing on the controversial theory called parental alienation syndrome. This was where abusive fathers, in more cases than people imagine, attempt to alienate the child against their mother in contested divorces. Not only did our reporting contradict the notion that women most often did the alienating in hotly contested situations but also that family courts were complicit in perpetuating the male power differential in these

Carmelita, Wade and Larry(l-r) at the Silver Circle Awards ceremony, November 15, 2006

cases. This circumstance played itself out recently on the HBO Max special about Woody Allen and Mia Farrow.

CPTV and Tatge-Lasseur were attacked unmercifully by men's advocacy groups casting doubt on our research and findings. PBS was ready to abandon the project as the pressure built.

Lee Newton, our national programming publicist, did a masterful job working to respond to the criticism, but it was punishing. We survived, the program was broadcast, and the din died down.

This controversy was in 2005, just before the true advent of the social media we know today. Had it occurred a few years later, I am convinced the program would have been pulled, denying the heartbreaking reality known to so many and placing in jeopardy the funding we received from the Mary Kay Ash Foundation.

The early to mid-2000s period had much to keep me occupied, but I was searching. There were nice moments, such as being inducted into the Boston/New England NATAS/Emmy group Silver Circle, the highest honor in New England television, in 2006.

And I would find a way to go on record about my growing disillusionment with the failings of the PBS system.

Chapter 40: "We're Starving PBS—and Our Future"

So read the headline in the July 5, 2004, editorial I penned for the public television system trade publication *Current*. My concerns about how we were organized as an industry had been building up for years. To that point, my only previous attempt at critiquing public television was satirical.

As a fan of Rob Bartlett's work on the *Imus in the Morning* radio program, I sought to use his gift for humor and social commentary in constructing *Rob Bartlett's Not for Profit T.V. Special* in 1995. In it, he poked fun at the public television industry for taking itself too seriously.

It was all very funny, but most memorable was the Ken Burns's send-up *Everything That's Happened…So Far*. Donning an early Beatles mop top, Rob, as Ken, told us that his beat on history would take us "from the big bang to Kurt Cobain. From the invention of white-out to the presidency of Millard Fillmore." The skit ended describing the collection just as another tape was rolling out of the edit suite.

I can imagine that many others in midcareer or later have seen much in their workplace or industry that needs reform and yet avoid the risk of putting themselves on the line by suggesting changes that affect their colleagues and friends. I decided, however, to speak out because the cause was worth it.

My piece began, "The common refrain within public television is that we don't have enough money to support our programming mission. I respectfully disagree." I went on to say, "Isn't it surprising to see, in stark budget figures, that this system, which spends close to $1.6 billion a year, is using less than $150 million a year of its own revenues on its major national programming service?"

In translation, that meant that less than 10 percent of the collective revenues of the PBS system were being spent on national programming.

Our overreliance on corporate funders was related to our own underfunding of our product. That was tragic and apparent in how few new series and risks on innovation we could make.

I added, "For many years we've laughed more than we've cried over the system's duplications, overlaps, fierce pride in localism, and tendency to defend local fiefdoms at this expense of the whole. I fear the last laugh will belong to companies selling the many cable channels, video games, and digital gadgets that compete for viewers' time."

Little did I know how dominant those digital platforms would become some sixteen years later with the multitude of high-quality streaming services now available.

At the time I spoke to the fact that while we still might have the best in many genres like natural history, do-it-yourself programs, science, documentary, and children's programming, full channels had developed around what we started. So why not declare victory and go home? We were pathfinders and pioneers who helped ensure that the "vast wasteland" concerns expressed by former FCC chairman Newton Minnow had been addressed.

What follows is what I got the most response from within the system.

I wrote, "It's as if our stations are community employment agencies, paralyzed by inertia and not willing to call the question: Is the system's present structure contributing to our demise? If so, how do we fix it?" I

*Larry and Carmelita at CPTV's 50th
Anniversary Gala in Hartford on 2013*

went on to recount a history that occluded our vision and ability to change as would be necessary given the pace of media evolution.

When President Johnson signed the Public Broadcasting Act into law in 1967, he proclaimed that he would figure out a permanent, reliable means of funding that provided insulation from politics. Then the politics of the Vietnam War ended his presidency, and that critical element was never addressed. What he left in place was an underfunded system of stations, one in virtually every congressional district, which is now well down the road past anachronistic.

In this moment, as we see the specter of growing consolidation of corporate ownership of media, the need for a well-funded and insulated public television system is greater than ever. In the 1980s, 90 percent of mass media was controlled by around fifty companies. Now that number of controlling corporations is fewer than ten.

If we are determined to have a sprawling public television system, as a nation, let us make a commitment to use that reach into forgotten parts of America—now called news deserts as advertising dollars for local newspapers and radio stations have disappeared in many places—to become a reliable source of news and information.

If CPTV, for example, had its operations in a small building in Hartford, just doing local and national programming and local underwriting and left all other membership and backroom functions to a regional hub, far more local programming would be possible, and a greater contribution could be made to PBS to experiment with new programming forms.

Some of that has occurred since I left the system but not nearly enough. Many more jobs must be shed, more station operations combined, and budgets pared from anything that the viewer cannot see on the screen. In my lengthy piece, I had more to say to system brethren. I will spare you.

Some people said I was spot-on with my analysis. Many others said nothing and "ob-la-di, ob-la-da, life goes on."

I share this because I sensed that the end of my wonderful time in the system was fast approaching, even if it proved to be a slow unwind. My whole identity was tied up in the place.

Most people thought that I would ultimately take Jerry Franklin's place as the president. He did not leave until 2019.

CPTV offered an early retirement package in mid-2009. Like most such packages, there were targets in mind. While I was eligible based on the criteria established, I was not one of them. I should have been. I had run out of gas. Part of that was my own inability to compete with the past, but there were external factors, such as a punishing recession, which reminded me that funding quality work with reputable people was going to get harder. In my view it is dangerous territory when the pace of change in the external world dwarfs your internal ability to keep pace. I had arrived at that place.

When I was introduced to a man who wanted to fund programming by using viaticals as the basis for the support and I entertained the idea, I knew it was time to go. Viaticals are instruments that use the purchase of life insurance policies as the seed corn for a continuous stream of funding. After all, if you purchase my $500,000 life insurance policy, pay me a portion, and keep up the premium, one day it is certain that that investment will pay off. I will die.

The fact that I even listened to this concept told me all I needed to know about what I had to do when the retirement package was offered.

I remember a development director early in Jerry's tenure telling me that I would never leave CPTV. For a while there, I thought he might be right.

My work at CPTV was the most meaningful and important assignment in my lifetime, yet I knew my work was done.

If you are a rainmaker, sometimes you lull yourself into thinking that there is more energy you can squeeze out of the clouds. I had more drenchings than I could ever have imagined. It was time to stop.

In my remarks to staff at a send-off party, I said that I had spent, by my accounting, fifty thousand hours working at CPTV over the years. I thanked my colleagues for giving me the room and support required to dream and attempt, fail and recover, and lose my way and find it again over this long stretch of time. After all, these were people with whom I celebrated the births of children, mourned the deaths of parents, and worked through the many changes from young adulthood to middle age.

I thanked many indispensable people that day, saving my most heartfelt appreciation for Lisa and the rare bond we had formed and the many travails we had survived. In her own earthy style, she captured it all best by saying, "Sorry I threw up a few times on the roller coaster." It was inevitable given the journey we shared together.

My route out was made easier when Jerry asked me to continue consulting on national programming through 2011. I also stayed on the air pledging UConn games and other programs, and I was about to head back to radio, my first love.

Chapter 41: Ed and Don

Given that I had been doing a talk program on the weekends since 2002, the idea of doing a daily program seemed appealing. How hard could it be? After all, the *Talk of the Town* program on WATR, which I knew might be coming available soon, was only fifteen hours a week on air.

I left CPTV in the spring of 2009 and did not start the daily program until early January 2010. I enjoyed this carefree interim period. While I was consulting for CPTV and doing my radio program on weekends, I was as unconstrained by schedule as I had ever been as an adult. I was given the opportunity to maintain my office at CPTV and move out at a leisurely pace. Given that my wife had a thriving physical therapy practice and I had the consulting dollars coming in, finances were not an issue.

APT honored me at an event in Florida in November 2009 for the volume of programming we had produced for that national service over the years. It was a bit unusual being at a system meeting but now approaching it from a distance. Carmelita came with me, and we did not attend many events while we were there. I had to separate. I had to come to grips with whether I could be as happy on a smaller stage—local radio—as I imagined I would be.

Thomas Wolfe's question of being able to return home again certainly lingered in my mind. The only way I could approach it was to vest a huge importance in finding my own voice and giving the listeners a different kind of listening experience.

While the market was small—about five hundred thousand throughout the reach of the signal—the station was classic, and the program was part of my hometown's history; it was a new palate altogether. It is one thing to be the impresario of programming that is the composite work of so many, and it is another to host and produce a program that really stands to be judged totally on your creativity. I had great role models.

Ed Flynn, who was the host of the program that I would take over, was my first program director at WWCO. He and I always got along well because as he recalls, I never broke format. That was important to him. With his New York roots and classic announcing style, Ed was a Connecticut broadcasting icon with successful stints in Bridgeport, New Haven, and Hartford. His morning show numbers in New Haven and Bridgeport were off the charts for those markets—and for other markets that size nationwide. His delivery was silky smooth, and he had a gift for the clever turn of the phrase in a compact way for maximum impact.

While he was a disc jockey's disc jockey, at WATR he was converted into a talk show host and had very definite opinions about politics. He and I disagreed on politics. It did not matter because I was in awe of his delivery and facility with the language. He built a devoted following.

Ed was always complimentary of what I did as a broadcaster, but I feared that his rabid conservative audience would not take to my more mainstream to liberal politics. I could also not emulate his combative style. While the name of the program has never changed over the years, the whole nature of the program and the audience is contoured by the tone of the host.

When I first decided that I would like to try my hand at this talk radio thing, I sat in a few times with a dear friend, Don Russell, on his program on WGCH in Greenwich. He was as close to a father figure as I had had since my dad's much too early passing.

Don's career in broadcasting was legendary. He was Stamford, Connecticut's, own but did stints at the Grand Ole Opry radio station in Nashville, on the national Monitor Radio in New York, and as Jackie Gleason's announcer on his first series *Cavalcade of Stars*, in which Don was the first person to introduce a sketch with the words "Now, ladies and gentlemen, "The Honeymooners". He regaled me with stories of the Gleason years. For example, I never realized that the Simon brothers, Neil and Danny, wrote for Gleason in the early days, but they never met him. Each script they delivered would be met with Gleason bellowing, "Leave it under the door!" And with an hour to fill on the live program, if the material was not timed properly, Jackie would say he was out of there and leave it to Don to fill the hole that existed with his capable reading of public service announcements. By the time Don finished, Jackie was well into the cups at the legendary Toots Shor's watering hole.

In his later years, Don came back to his hometown of Stamford, perhaps giving me permission to feel that was okay to do too. He served as an opinion columnist for the *Stamford Advocate*, as the morning man and talk show host on various stations, and in his final years, as the general manager of a small operation CPTV ran out of the Rich Forum in downtown Stamford.

Jerry hired Don because of his name in town as we still attempted to wrest viewers from WNET in New York with the difficult assignment of turning Fairfield County's residents from being culturally New Yorkers into culturally Connecticuters. Despite the huge impact of UConn women's basketball, it remained an ongoing battle. Don had a mismatched ensemble working there, and the effort was ill-fated from the start, but I enjoyed spending days with him trying to jump-start projects that could be housed there.

I enjoyed most our conversations at lunches at the City Limits Diner in Stamford and our musings about the business. We were often joined by Ron Ropiak, an experienced producer who did many business-related programs for CPTV given his history producing material for General Electric over the years.

By this point Don was in his eighties, and his energy to do what was required against so many odds had diminished. But his memory and love for the business never lagged.

He was so pleased to encourage his old friend Art Carney to join us at the studios to tape thirty minutes of stories about working with Gleason for a documentary we hoped to produce. Funding for the documentary never materialized; however, spending time with these two legends was more than gratifying as they played off each other, reflecting on a historic relationship in the golden years of television.

As in the tragic case of Andrew Jones, Don's passing in 2010 hit me hard. It was like losing my dad all over again.

Don was a man of the past, the present, and always the future, particularly sold on the prospects for his hometown. The *New York Times* piece on his passing stated, "With an unaffected, casual style, Mr. Russell would tell his listeners about the wondrous sunrise they probably had missed or the storm that was brewing. He also would reminisce about 'old Stamford' and, unlike many of his contemporaries, praised the city's downtown redevelopment and its emergence as a headquarters site for many major corporations."

While both Ed Flynn and Don were broadcast legends I have embraced as colleagues and friends, my emerging radio style, less abrasive and more hopeful, would emulate the influence Don had on me.

Chapter 42: My World of Talk Radio Doesn't Exist

Opinion radio has become a junkyard for rants, diatribes, conspiracists, and malcontents. And those are just the callers. Many of the hosts are worse.

I had to ask myself why I wanted to try my hand at something I was so miscast for to begin with. How could I bring civility, education, and high purpose to the craft, clearly a different formula, and stay on the air for any length of time?

My first challenge was a ubiquitous caller who went by the pseudonym Ferris. While others seemed open to a more welcoming voice, one not marinated in the anger and outrage that most hosts applied liberally to their conservatism, this man had a new outrage daily. He had an agile mind and clear delivery, punctuated by one invective after another—"9/11 was an inside job" or "Seat belts are a violation of my constitutional rights." He was the embodiment of the whole panoply of grievances that predated the soon-arriving Trump era.

I would go back and forth with him, ready to play the straight man to what seemed to me had to be schtick. He called every talk show in Con-

Larry at 1320 WATR hosting 'Talk of the Town'

necticut yet seemed to relish the thoughtful pushback I offered.

While I engaged with him and others of the same stripe, my vision was of a highly produced program with many guests and lively discussion. What I lacked in vitriol, I made up in pace and thoughtfulness. This prescription worked in this market, primarily because I added to the core audience. Tom Chute often heard from women who now found it tolerable to occupy the war zone of talk radio.

I envisioned the show as being like a public square—but one without floggings and beatings. I really wanted to raise the discourse in my hometown, and like my dad, I wanted to make a difference for my beleaguered city. That translated into meticulous preparation, guest recruitment beyond the confines of most local market programs exhibiting a wide range of views, and a more expansive view of the subject matter. While not confident that I could please some who wanted the more combative style, I was certain that I could make a broader array of topics interesting to a larger audience.

In October 2008, more than a year before I took my weekend program to a daily platform, I described what my approach would be in an article published in the bible of talk radio, *Talkers Magazine*, the brainchild of Michael Harrison, who once had his own talk show on WTIC in Hartford. In what was titled "A Case for Nonpartisan Talk Radio," I opened in the following manner: "I live in a world of talk radio that doesn't exist. The experts say it cannot. A lively host with fully informed opinions and a willingness to defend them, even though they stand against the bipolarity of the American spectrum. Is that possible?" I went on to say that I invite guests with views outside the political mainstream, agree with them on some issues, and contest others, just as most of us do in real life.

I used to attend the *Talkers Magazine* seminar held annually in New York City just to hear speaker after speaker telling me that what I was doing could not be successful. Perhaps in a larger market, they were right. I thought I understood mine as a nearly lifelong resident, and I would bet my reputation as an editorialist that I could pull it off.

I recall Bill Bennett, the former education secretary and an author, decrying at one of the seminars that talk show hosts were often too simplistic, and they should be required to do an internship in government to see how it really works. I was reminded that my stint at the Connecticut Department of Education was that for me and the wider aperture of content I assembled and produced at CPTV brought me to a different place than the path others had traveled to sit behind that mic.

Looking back, I had a lot of temerity telling grizzled hosts that they might gain more insights by reading a novel from time to time for true wisdom about the human condition and our times. By the way, I referred to another favorite novel, Walter Mosley's *The Man in My Basement*, if they had the desire to ponder questions of a philosophical nature. I further opined that my listeners might have to listen right up until Election Day to find out who I was voting for or that I might just give them the facts and let them make up their own minds. I even suggested that I could hold two competing notions at the same time and feel comfortable with the competition of ideas going on in my mind.

In offering to sell them a service where I told them who to vote for and promise to provide them with a detailed, thoughtful rationale for their vote preference, sharable with friends, I was trying to say that the superficiality of preference is unfortunate.

In suggesting that our city of broadcast origin should house a Museum of Political Corruption, since that was a moniker we earned for a reason, I put public figures on notice that this "sheriff" was going to be attentive to misdeeds.

During my stint as the town crier, I wanted to play various roles—the city's most attentive citizen, wise guide, healer, provocateur, and comfortable voice. Someone you had to tune in to every day because the robust dialogue was something you would not want to miss.

It is somewhat ironic that the station, having been home to more acerbic and confrontative hosts in the past, was forced to install a security system on my watch. Honesty itself can return vicious pushback. When I criticized the process of a city hire, based on nepotism more than competence and appropriateness for the job, the father of the man came to the then unsecured facility looking for me. I had left for the day, so instead he let his ire out on Barbara Davitt, the fabled host of *Coffee Talk*, an over fifty-year legend at the station.

Like every previous assignment, I wanted to leave it all on the field, make an indelible contribution, and exit before I had exhausted my passion. Little did I realize at first how much work that represented.

While I had producers assigned to the program, the first, the late Alan Todd, was very helpful, but he often could not keep up with the pace I was setting for the program. Therefore, I got into the early habit of booking large segments of the program myself. Instead of trying to convey what I wanted the show to be like or what story I read in one of the many newspapers I consumed daily, I would just do it myself.

Alan's great contribution to the program was getting me one of the many A-list guests we had on over time. He had been friendly with Henry Winkler when they both attended Emerson College in Boston. Henry was promoting a new book on learning about life through his time on the river and love of flyfishing. He is such a gentleman and wonderful conversationalist.

My second producer, Frank Marro, was also the news director at the station. He was simpatico with what I was trying to do with the program but only had so much time and energy to give me the support I required to make the three-hour program what I wanted. We drew lines, and he booked a few slots, and I filled in the others.

Given Frank's extensive news background in radio and television, we did our best work together on the day of the tragic school shooting at Sandy Hook in Newtown, Connecticut, which was in our listening area. His news judgment about the fragments of information coming in as the tragedy was unfolding in real time, careful not to get ahead of the story, was invaluable. My instincts were always to be cautious until we could source information properly.

I can vividly recall that the devastation of precious young lives occurred on a Friday, and we had a program already built for Monday. I scrapped the entire program and rebuilt it over the weekend with guests germane to the topic of this shooting and the spate of massacres in the country. I watched CNN and then reached out to an author I saw who had much to say and fortunately was able to continue to secure such guests on more occasions than I should have given our reach.

Some of the most important moments I spent on air were in times of distress for the community. My manner was more soothing than abrasive and had a calming influence. I played counterpoint to the default position of many other hosts. In looking back at my dad's most important broadcast moment, it was likely his three-day stint on air helping Waterbury through its greatest natural calamity, the Flood of 1955. It was much in my mind as an unusual winter-like Halloween northeaster battered the region in

October 2011, which some called Shocktober, and took out all essential services when I was able to go on air for a seven-hour stretch with no notion of what we could offer except a familiar voice. One by one calls came in from various city officials and citizens giving pieces of the emerging storm response to hungry listeners.

My third producer was Jon Krofssik, who is a broadcast engineer by training but not in mood or tone. Rather than gruff and resistant, Jon was gentle and responsive. From the minute I started at WATR, Jon was at the ready if I needed any assistance. We became fast friends.

While Jon was jack-of-all-trades already at the station, he was more than willing to sign on as producer when Frank left to go South. He wanted to run with me as I insisted that the program be timely, relevant, and thoughtful every day. And he never minded when I overrode something he had scheduled because I found something just a bit more important for the next day. It was a great partnership that has remained into the next phase of my career in podcasting.

My goal was to elevate the level of discourse for listeners. Did I succeed? Could I point to real-life impact? Time would tell.

Chapter 43: I Got This

A December 15, 2013, article in the *Republican-American* stated, "After a week of withering public criticism, the (Waterbury) Board of Aldermen abandoned its parliamentary attempt to limit who can speak at meetings, and for how long."

The foiled attempt to suppress speech would have prohibited the public from talking about topics that were not on the agenda and from making what were deemed personal attacks. The new rules would have also limited speech on the part of the aldermen themselves.

I perceived my role as a talk show host not simply to agitate, as most were more skilled than me at doing, but also to instigate change and promote new ways of thinking about issues.

When the new rules were adopted a week earlier, I went on the air chastising the actions as heavy-handed and irresponsible. My listeners followed suit, and the effective unrest about these actions began. It took one week to restore speaking privileges to both the citizens and the aldermen.

In the same year, the issue of representation on the board of aldermen itself took centerstage. Previous attempts at changing the way aldermen were elected had failed.

The city of Waterbury, while changing demographically, was politically still in the hands of white citizens from wealthier neighborhoods and was effectively run from the mayor's office. With a strong mayor system and an "at-large" election of aldermen, generally the majority on the board was made up of members of the mayor's party. What he said was passed by the majority on the board.

In the past, the issue of district election of aldermen replacing "at-large" election had its greatest support in underrepresented areas of the city, including brown and black neighborhoods. I felt that the issue was one of fairness. Waterbury had developed a strong neighborhood council, so people in communities throughout the city were developing strategies to improve their neighborhoods. From such groups could come the talent pool to fill vacancies on the board of aldermen. This would wrest control from the mayor's office.

Over time I developed a good relationship with the then, and still, mayor of the city, Neil O'Leary, as I had his predecessor, Michael Jarjura. After two previous mayors had been convicted and sentenced to jail time, Waterbury was being led by people who seemed to have their priorities straight.

Institutional change should never be made assuming the best from unchecked power. The legislative function in the city needed to go from a rubber stamp to an involved body, responsible to a smaller portion of the electorate, who could keep tabs on their actions. After all, that is how we elect legislators at other levels of government.

Over the years I grew more aware of the functioning of this board as their meetings were carried on public access every other Monday. My wife could not believe that through the haze of poor production values, I would dutifully sit down and watch the entire proceeding. I felt it was my job. It gave me plenty of fodder for the next day's program. And I enjoyed the hurly-burly of local politics.

While for years I was living on the air of a statewide and national programming platform, now I was enjoying the roots of planting myself back in my hometown and using my skills to affect change that I could sense in the community.

I kept thinking about one of my favorite songwriters, and twice a guest on my program, the incomparable Jimmy Webb. He had written songs such as "MacArthur Park," "Wichita Lineman," "By the Time I Get to Phoenix," and so many others. There's an argument to be made that he was the Gershwin of my generation. He also wrote a song, "If You See Me Getting Smaller I'm Leaving," which I would use as the basis for justifying my contentment in coming home and stepping down from the higher ground I once stood on. The line that stood out for me was "I have the right to disappear."

An old friend of mine, a fine newsman in radio and for the state's Associated Press, now deceased, Steve Feica, was none too charitable when he said to me, "Larry, why are you feeding pearls to the swine?" I never felt that way. I came to find out that there were many in the audience so appreciative of a show that took the dialogue up a few notches. They had been waiting for someone who challenged them to think about issues in a different way.

The idea that a talk show could have an impact on a long simmering issue of representation in a city might have been fanciful. However, I took the conversation from its previous place of black versus white to fairness versus unfairness. All neighborhoods needed a voice. The board should be made up of those who cared about their fellow citizens, not those who would do the bidding of the mayor—many of whom had let the entire city down in the past.

To the shock of many, the referendum to change the way aldermen were selected passed by a few thousand votes. Talk is cheap, yet purposeful words do matter. Was the show and my advocacy decisive in the process? There is no way to know conclusively, but it was the one variable that had changed over the many attempts to do this. The "by district" election method adopted is by no means perfect. It is a bridge to more reform going forward, but for our city, it was a big step forward.

I used the show to debate key issues and always took center stage as the moderator of debates every election cycle. I was viewed as a fair arbiter who challenged the candidates to be prepared or prepare to be embarrassed. I remember one city department head, who was reluctant at first to appear and came with a phalanx of aides, told me after numerous interviews that I made him better at his job. He had to think through his actions, knowing I would hold him to account down the road.

I made friends with major publishers, authors, think tanks, and individuals and populated the program with the likes of Ralph Nader, Mario Cuomo, Alan Dershowitz, Phil Donahue, and other well-known public personalities. People wondered how I wrangled guests of this type. My simple answer was "I asked them." Most assumed it was by way of my contacts at CPTV. That was not the case.

I would run the program more like a magazine, going from hard news to softer features, often about the music business. You might tune in and hear Jimmy Webb, Tommy James, or the man who made Muscle Shoals the legendary venue to record for artists as diverse as R&B, the Delta blues, and the Rolling Stones. Or you might stumble upon the producer of the documentary on the legendary Wrecking Crew, a group of A-list musicians who backed major acts in Hollywood throughout the 1960s.

I set up debates between dueling experts on various subjects and let them have at it, such as Gerald Posner and Dr. Jerome Corsi on the Kennedy assassination.

I could be playful at times too. I went out looking to do a series of interviews with Connecticut people with whom I shared my name. The *Larry Rifkin Interviews Larry Rifkin* series kicked off with the deputy editor of the *Jerusalem Post*, who was originally from Bloomfield, Connecticut, and at one time was a stringer for CBS News. He would often get confused for me in people's minds. In truth, it was me just moving around in my early career. Dr. Larry Rifkin, a Hartford area physician, turned out to be an expert on Darwin and traveled around the world to validate his work.

I got the most umbrage when I brought on a Trump impersonator, John DiDomenico, during the campaign in 2016. A favorite of Howard Stern and many others, he not only got the voice down, but he was also hilarious in his understanding of Trump's psyche.

Everything we did was unrehearsed, and yet he was remarkably adept on his feet. I asked him if he would decorate the White House, like other Trump properties, and he said that there would be a fountain, of course, "filled with the tears of losers, like Ted Cruz and Jeb Bush." I said some of us might consider voting for Trump if we knew Melania would be around for all four years. He said, "Larry, you know me well, forty-four and out the door." I invited my listeners to call in and talk to Donald Trump, thinking they got the joke. Many did not. They called after I ended the conversation. When I broke the news to some, they were so angry at me. If they thought that was the real Donald Trump, given the satirical nature of the questions and answers, I knew that was a disturbing sign.

My most popular feature was the twice yearly *Way Back Waterbury*, where I would bring in a panel of my favorite Waterburians and invite conversation about the old days downtown and around the city. The phones lit up, and the memories began to flow. People wanted me to do it more often, but we had discussed the same city theaters, restaurants, and landmarks so many times over the many years of doing it that I thought twice a year kept it special.

My dear friend P. J. Conway, a former sportswriter at the *Republican-American*, was a guest on virtually every *Way Back Waterbury* show I did, as were Ron Diorio, a former major league pitcher from the city, and musician Bob Mobilio, the owner of the store where I took drum lessons. Others would come pass through, such as the remarkable educator and sports official Norm Feitelson, but they were the regulars.

Larry with co-host, Tom Hill, at a 1320 WATR remote broadcast

One of the saddest moments during the pandemic was the send-off for beloved P. J. at a service where we could only wave to his wonderful family as we drove by.

Throughout my time on air, I developed interesting relationships with statewide leaders, most particularly with Gov. Dannel P. Malloy, the former mayor of Stamford. More importantly, he had been the attorney for Don Russell, and they had a great friendship. For that reason, I felt kindly toward him. Aside from that, he was one of the smartest people I ever interviewed and forced me to be better at my job. I prepared more for interviews with him than virtually any guest.

When he joined me for the first time, seeking his first term in office, he could see that I was a different kind of talk host. He complimented me on air as someone who "does the job the way it should be done." I think he meant fairly and down the middle.

Every year after his budget address, he would come on my program to explain it. After he signed on to a budget proposal with a tax increase in 2015—having promised not to do so in his second run for office—we had a bruising conversation on air. I was upset with him, and it showed. The public loved my combative style in that interview. To me, I was just trying to hold him to account.

While we talked less often in the ensuing years, he made it a point to call me on my last day on the air in January 2017 to say that he appreciated the work. It was a gesture of respect, which I greatly appreciated.

I had an interesting relationship with Chris Murphy, who was the congressman from our district when I started and later became a respected and rising US senator. The day the House of Representatives was voting on the Affordable Care Act, I asked if he would come on with us and explain his vote in favor. His office said that he could only come on at 9:50 a.m. for ten minutes. They knew I did not go on the air until 10:00 a.m. I said yes to taping the interview, a rarity, and I was uncertain about the Rube Goldberg–type legislation, still not convinced that it would be what we needed, given the industry influence needed to push it through.

Over the years he grew into his job, and I believe I did as well. Our many subsequent conversations were healthy exchanges on a range of issues.

On my departure, his handwritten note said, "We will miss your voice, and your common sense, on the airwaves. Make sure to keep in touch, okay?" Did I? Have we? No, but that is immaterial. I knew the sentiment was genuine.

And finally, on a few occasions, I broke the news.

I described my warm personal relationship with former governor John Rowland, once imprisoned for improprieties in office. When he came out of prison, he became a talk show host in Hartford on the state's most respected outlet, WTIC-AM.

But John was a creature of Waterbury. He came back to live in the area, though interestingly, when first released from prison, he stayed temporarily at Frank Luntz's home in West Hartford. This is the same man who more recently let Kevin McCarthy stay at one of his expensive pads in Washington, DC.

By the way, the now-famous pollster made his first television appearance ever on CPTV. Years back, his dad had called me to say that his son was underground with then dissident Lech Wałęsa, and he would be smuggling tapes out of Poland. He asked if I would be interested in designing a program including this rare footage. If you've read this far, you might imagine I said yes, and the Emmy-nominated *Walesa Tapes* was aired.

How could I say no to Dr. Lester Luntz, a respected forensic dentist, whose lifelong passion was Hitler's teeth?

While John Rowland began his first stint out of a prison away from the Waterbury area, he wanted to be thought of most kindly, despite indiscretions, by the folks in his hometown. He knew the type of talk show host I was, and if I saw disturbing behavior, I would report on it.

He got caught up in political malfeasance a second time by secretly working for a candidate for Congress with the money flowing through her family's rehabilitation business. He was said to be a consultant to that business and not her campaign as she did not want that to be a point of contention in her race for Congress. Furthermore, he used WTIC's airwaves to denigrate one of her primary opponents without the public knowing of his backhanded compensation.

To make a sordid tale short, I was appalled at WTIC being used in this manner and had some inside information that he was going to be indicted. I went out on a limb in divulging this information before other outlets. It was a huge story for Waterbury.

During this period he asked a fellow host to have me back off on the air. The other host told him to talk to Tom Chute. He never did. Postscript: John did another tour in a federal penitentiary. We have not spoken since. I understand that he has been trying to pull things together, and I wish him no malice. I hope he appreciates that I was just doing my job.

In my last few months on the air, the Waterbury Neighborhood Council gave me an award for service to the city as a voice for informed local conversation.

So why did I leave after seven years?

First, I never expected to stay that long. As hard as I worked at CPTV, I think this position was the most all-consuming of my career. I would wake up every morning scouring the internet for material, go in about an hour before the show, leave an hour later only to go home and prepare for the next day, and seek out more topics and people. It never stopped.

Second, frankly, I wanted nothing to do with Donald Trump and his soon-to-be misadventures in office. I might have been the first commentator anywhere to state up front, after he was elected but before he took the oath of office, that he would be impeached. My audience was apoplectic. How can you say this? I said that he had no knowledge of government, had never reported to a board of directors, and was a loose cannon, and if anyone could bump into corners in an Oval Office, it was him. I never thought he would go beyond my horrified projection and hit the impeachment daily double.

Today I admire many commentators on TV and radio who have staffs aplenty and larger platforms doing what I attempted to do every day with a part-time producer. I had no luxury to bask in a good show because I had to reset and prepare to come back with a chock-full three hours the next day.

At age sixty-four, that was it. I wanted to move on.

Kevin Rennie—a guest many times on the program, a former state senator, and now a weekly opinion columnist for the *Hartford Courant*—in his blog *Daily Ructions*, captured it succinctly. The headline says, "Larry Rifkin to Begin Third Act, Leaving Daily Radio at WATR." He went on, "Larry Rifkin will be taking his great big brain into more relaxing pursuits than what daily talk radio requires. The WATR veteran has been at his Waterbury post for seven years, more than he planned when he joined the station after a storied career in Connecticut public broadcasting. This is not the last we will hear from the honey-voiced talker. He will be filling in and doing remotes for WATR. Larry will also begin dabbling in the expanding world of podcasting. He will also be volunteering at CRIS Radio. Whatever he does, Larry will continue to be a reasonable and interesting voice in the world that often feels like it has lost its way."

I had a plan for this next stage. Could it be as satisfying as all the others? The late Larry King said that being behind a mic is the one thing in his life that never let him down. For all who have been involved, as a vocation or for fun in college or as a dalliance, it is always remembered as the sweetest and most alluring of mistresses.

Chapter 44: Stepping Back but Not Away from the Mic

Saying goodbye in a very public job is tough. Maybe that's the reason the US Senate looks like a nursing home for the powerful and influential. Or professional athletes stay a season or two beyond their high impact point.

I am reminded by my wife that giving up her great physical therapy practice was tough on her as she said goodbye to patients and staff. I get it. Moving on is tough in any event.

What was difficult for me to explain to people was why, even though I still had the energy and the drive, I just felt it was enough. I really did not want to be on the air a day longer than the hard-to-define "best use by" date. When I began to fade at CPTV, it was at the desk and never on the air.

At my talk show post, it would have been right out in the open. I had a dear friend in the business who literally came in to do a shift while on his deathbed and another who management recalled stopped getting calls because he had grown so combative and surly in response to callers.

It is always best to leave them wanting more. Besides I had a plan. I called it my February file. It was my plan for when I went from working full time to what I call casual employment, on my own terms.

I hate the word "retirement." In a recent version of *Merriam-Webster* dictionary, the term was said to mean "to disappear," "to go away," and "to withdraw." It connotes lack of purpose and drive, and I still had both. I just wanted to apply those attributes to my own pursuits.

Did you ever notice that in this society, we are relegated to the back bench, to a new status of insignificance when we cannot answer the question "So what do you do?" The value America places on work and career explains the lack of definition around the value of other pursuits, such as stay-at-home parenting and caregiving for all generations.

In other cultures, when people have arrived at a certain age, they are revered and venerated for what they have achieved. The wisdom they have attained through the art of living a long life is sought after by generations that follow.

And if you stop to reflect, simply surviving intact should be a marker of some status. How many people have you seen who, by virtue of bad decisions or bad luck, lost their way along the road well ahead of you, no matter the gifts they started out with?

I have begun to look at life as a game of subtraction. Most of us start out with a high degree of mental acuity and many physical gifts, and one by one they are stripped away. Just look at an old photograph of yourself as a reminder. The new goal should be to hold to as many as you can for as long as you can.

I have generally lived a life of the mind. My body has very few miles on it. It has been beneficial that I got into an exercise routine years back and am disciplined to a fault. The over eleven thousand miles on my current treadmill is a marker to that habit. Nothing fancy but four miles, slow pace, every day. My doctor, with a practice made up of many retired factory workers, is always glad to see me because I have none of the scars and ailments borne of a life of grueling, repetitive work under very marginal conditions from past indifference or ignorance by employers.

I arrived at this moment fully intact. What would I do with the good fortune? While I like recreation, I still love the work. My goal was to do what I love on my own terms.

In that "February file" was the intention to volunteer for CRIS Radio, a reading service for the visually impaired in our state. Until COVID-19, I would head down to a great little studio at the University of New Haven once or twice a week and do a live read of copy from the *New Haven Register* for forty minutes straight. Oh, yes, copy that was written to be read, not uttered. It is harder than it looks, even for a broadcast veteran. I developed a goal of a read with no mistakes. I never got there until I began doing the reads as recordings from home twice a week during the pandemic. Recently I did one with not a stutter or gaffe of any sort. While volunteering satisfied my desire to play radio and do a service for others, I needed to feel like I was still in the game.

With my partner, Jon Krofssik, I developed a podcast based on a passion I had for a topic area that gave me flexibility.

When I was on radio, I loved to introduce my listeners to where our society and politics were headed, so I would find authors who were writing about those trends. Thus, America Trends podcast (americatrendspodcast.com) was born, and it's "where the future has arrived, and it's just in time." We tackle subjects that interest me. For example:

"What will a decreasing baby population mean for our society going forward?"

"Have the delivery economy and online retailers destroyed brick-and-mortar sellers for good?"

"Why are Americans walking away from organized religion at such a stunning rate?"

"Why are our politics becoming more divisive? What can we do about it?"

"What impact will legalizing marijuana have on the criminal justice system?"

"Why is the military having a hard time meeting its recruitment goals?"

"Will climate change make parts of America uninhabitable over time?"

"How do you know if you are a political hobbyist, and what does this voyeurism, from afar, achieve or excuse?"

"Where will your office be in the future now that the pandemic is subsiding?"

By choosing to focus on subjects that were not temporal and would not go stale if they were not posted with immediacy, it gave me the flexibility to record in advance and on my own schedule. We recruited a social media designer, the capable Scott Phillips, who worked with me at CPTV. He was most aware of the consistency required to make this more than a hobby.

So I ran with the podcast as my way of staying stimulated and in the game, without being absorbed by it. We had a goal of posting two podcasts a week, and at the outset we did our recording in a production studio at WATR.

Tom Chute was gracious in letting us do this. In return I made myself available for spot assignments on remote broadcasts for the station. Ultimately I took to recording the podcast back home using an app on my phone.

Jon and Scott gave me a great team, which helped me achieve the modest goals I set out for myself.

Podcasting is now becoming a real challenger to conventional radio, except its fragmentation means few podcasts really rise to levels of mass consumption.

The last statistic I read indicated there are 1.5 million podcasts. Some are indulgences with two sports fanatics doing five episodes and then quitting. Others are very niche and still others proprietary. The major players are associated with NPR, the *New York Times*, Spotify, iHeart, and other services that built up in this new era, and others became their own brands, such as Gimlet Media. True crime and the success of the progenitor of this genre, *Serial*, set a standard for the industry.

In my case, I just wanted to continue having a reason to read terrific books, interview smart people, maintain my relationship with publishers, and stay in touch with where we were headed in this disorienting time.

We started out in the spring of 2017 in earnest, months after I left radio, with three specific goals: to get on all major aggregator sites such as Apple and Spotify, get picked up by a network, and attain a sponsor.

While revenues for podcasts in 2020 rose an estimated 48 percent to $708 million and are projected to exceed $1 billion in 2021, those entities with sponsorship are still a small percentage of the universe of podcasts.

As of this writing, we have recorded over 470 podcasts, got picked up in 2019 by the mental health news radio network (mhnrnetwork.com), and were one of only 75,000 podcasts picked up by Amazon as the newest player in the aggregator field (though I have no idea why except our consistency). We attained a sponsor briefly in 2020 with a New England–based consulting firm BlumShapiro but lost them at the end of the year because of the pandemic. Despite the current lack of a sponsor, I keep recording two or more podcasts a week.

With hundreds of thousands, not millions, of listeners each year, it gives me great pleasure and keeps me stimulated. Some friends play golf every other day; Jon and I record, edit, and distribute our podcast.

I used the podcast as a discussion launch for a course I taught for two terms at the Osher Lifelong Learning Institutes (OLLI) at the University of Connecticut campus in Waterbury, where I was also a student.

I became involved with the Connecticut Community Foundation, the Connecticut Humanities, and local libraries and began moderating panels on the topic of "fake news" and other subjects germane to our region.

And I once again donned my consultancy robes, preparing a "bible" to lay out the tenets of *The Full Story*, Fairfield County's WSHU, the public radio affiliate's first talk show. At my urging, they hired Ron Ropiak to host it. It was short-lived as funding dried up, but my reacquaintance with Ron alone was worth the time spent in developing. I even recorded an NPR *StoryCorps* episode with then congresswoman Elizabeth Esty of Connecticut.

This was my plan to "step back but not away from the mic." At the same time, I started thinking back on this career and penning this reflection.

Twice asked to return to CPTV in the period after leaving, I balked. And recently when asked to return to daily radio, I similarly refused. I look upon this period of "casual employment" as fluid and ever changing.

The things that keep me feeling engaged in the moment may exhaust themselves, and I must be prepared to look for other pursuits in which to engage.

My constant companions, my wife and my drums; our children nearby; and one beautiful granddaughter, Zoey Dana, have been augmented now by the most adorable rescue dog, Lucy Kate, and a keyboard.

As a drummer, I always marveled at my bandmates as they spoke their own language while I tried to hold steady the time. I wanted to learn another instrument and thought that piano would be best for the desire I had, which was to put what I learned from reading Jimmy Webb's classic on the art of songwriting, *Wordsmith*, to work. I ventured to teach myself, primarily through pianogenius.com, enough keyboard skills to write my own songs. It was the one online course that met me directly where I was. The founder, Tim Gross, does an excellent job walking the adult learner through the process. My dad wrote songs, but he recorded none of his music, so he could not share his gift.

I was determined to at least record demos of my material and leave songs behind so that they are not gone with me. To date, I have recorded forty of them at Ace Tone Studios in Bethany, the next town over, with owner and engineer, Matt Terribile. What fun we have and what a joy I have of writing about love and whatever else speaks to me as a topic for verse and melody.

I saw a four-car funeral one day and imagined what that said about the life of that person and put it to song in "Four Cars." I watched the dramatic HBO series on Chernobyl and wrote about the sacrifices of miners sent on a mission that was sure to lead to their early deaths and described what I was feeling in "For the Others." I saw on *The Crown* the dramatization of the plight of the man who broke into Buckingham Palace because no one else would listen to his sad tale of a life gone off the rails, so I wrote "Speak to the Queen." I read an account of Jennifer Dulos, a slain mother in Connecticut, and her youthful days in New York City and wrote "Party Girl" to recount.

I took a course at OLLI on the great composers and was fascinated with Beethoven given the fact that he wrote so much of his later work while being deaf and loved to compose in his head while taking long walks. That was my inspiration for the song "Walking with Beethoven." I sent it to the instructor, Dr. Vincent DeLuise, the cultural ambassador for the Waterbury Symphony Orchestra, and he loved the song.

And I composed a duet that my wife and I recorded called "I Was Out There Looking For You (and You Were Out There Looking For Me Too)." I've composed three other songs reflective of our relationship—"Partner of Light," "Old Love," and "Magic." I'm sure there will be more.

I am consumed by this new form of communication—lyric and melody. The construction of every three-minute composition takes so much time and care. Sometimes it feels right from the start. Other times it is a painful birth.

Are the songs good? Who knows? Judge for yourself at soundcloud.com or bandcamp.com, where I have posted a few. It is just me and the keys. Listener alert: I'm not a great singer and did not take up piano until I was sixty-four, so please judge on a curve. When I got notices from SoundCloud that two young women put "Party Girl" on their favorites list, it made my day. Their list was composed of new indie music and hip-hop.

It may be best that anyone doing this for fun does not fall into the "Mr. Tanner" trap. He is the character Harry Chapin built out of an account he read about an advertising man from Connecticut who loved to sing opera for himself. He was discovered and invited to sing at the Met. In a review, the *New York Times* skewered his performance in just two lines, and he stopped singing, even for his own enjoyment, for a long time after that. Finally, he regained his voice but would never subject himself to that scrutiny again.

Music is personal, and these songs mean something to me. Full stop.

While I have bandmates who put the pursuit of our music of cover songs from the 1960s and 1970s on hold, with our last gig out on Saturday, March 7, 2020, as the pandemic asserted itself, I would never ask them to play what I write. That can be the impetus for a band breakup.

Ed Flynn, the masterful broadcaster I alluded to earlier, says he wants the following on his tombstone: "He finally shut up."

For this moment in time, I am trying my hand at more modes of expression than ever.

With the concerns of making a living behind me and my health still good, I am free to enjoy this moment and afraid to squander it.

Epilogue

"After all, I'm not done yet." Pardon me as I borrow a phrase from a song lyric I composed. Although, admittedly, I am close.

This is a moment in time that belongs to someone savvy with technology, brimming with greater energy, and filled with dreams waiting to be fulfilled.

Blessed with a wonderful set of parents, a great partner, and a family of my own, I truly have had all that one man could ask for.

I have been engaged in pursuits that were enriching and gratifying and, at times, terrifying.

Amy Chua, a professor at Yale Law School, the author of *Battle Hymn of the Tiger Mother*, and twice a guest on my radio program, summed up my feelings perfectly.

She was quoted saying, "Everything precious in my life is something I was almost too scared to do."

I have gained enough wisdom along the way to know that my gifts are in no way extraordinary. My discipline and will to succeed are the two attributes the reader might most want to emulate. I can say I delivered them to the best of my abilities. As I end the telling of my journey, I am left with the unsettling question, who will claim that future in my industry?

Mainstream media outlets are on the run as they are being outflanked by online imitators, some who are assiduous in their work product while others look to attract views, clicks, engagements, and revenues through the purposeful design of incendiary content. I fear it may become the domain of editorialists and communicators much angrier and intentionally disruptive who resemble nothing of the traditions of public broadcasting, which mirrored those of commercial pathfinders like Edward R. Murrow. Our society is roiling, and reasonable voices and considered judgment are dismissed as old school.

Only a deliberate effort to undermine the reliability and accuracy of mainstream media outlets allows the lies and illogic of our moment to fester.

My small contribution was always meant to be constructive and designed to advance, not blunt. I was always committed to making a difference in the place where I lived. That was the legacy of my father and the mantle I wanted to assume.

The heritage broadcasting outlets are among the long-standing institutions fading as the digital space erases our geography and, with it, media accountability.

Today local newspaper and electronic media outlets struggle to engage people in their community as the economics of the business grow more difficult by the day, and the competitors for eyes and ears are remote and unfiltered and highlight the most malignant aspects of our culture.

If you see voting and civic engagement erode in your city or town, its corollary is a withering local news presence. The carnival atmosphere never took hold in the media town I lived in, and the

Larry at CPTV studios

junk food media diet was something I worked to avoid.

Video production and storytelling are currently everyone's domain. The smart phone has made it so. Given the universe now engaged in the arts and sciences of production, there is a devaluing of content. It is everywhere, and it is being designed by the skilled and the unskilled, the well intentioned and the nefarious.

The gatekeeper or curator, the programmer, is lost in the process. And that was me.

I am pleased to say that when I left that guardianship position and went on the front lines of talk radio and podcasting, I maintained those same editorial standards that have always guided me. I do believe that my ability to hold two divergent truths at the same time comes into play here.

While there is a greater quantity of bad video being marketed than ever before, I think it is fair to say with the advent of streaming services, there is also a greater quantity of excellent content than ever before.

On the audio side, it is interesting to me that the newfound strength of satellite radio and the emergence of podcasting now give listeners so many more quality choices just in the moment when much of terrestrial radio, exempting NPR in that category, has lost its way.

I note that with the volume of content now being offered by podcasters, wholly unregulated and personally sourced, there is little reference to this rapidly expanding industry when people disparage the devolution of content they find elsewhere. What are we to make of this?

When I was growing up in Waterbury, there were four radio stations in the local market, and each of the three-hour daily shifts was filled by local talent. Today, in this same market, there is one local outlet with just two announcing shifts a day. The question as to where young talent now goes may be the answer as to why podcasting offers so many promising options. After all, its cost of entry is so low.

As sponsorship becomes more attractive, more purveyors maintain standards to attract those previously scarce dollars.

I toiled in the media field when a few of us controlled the content that many would see and hear.

Now you, the listener and viewer, are in control. The choices are many, and the judgment required to find the good stuff rests in your hands.

I will continue to look for ways to put my aging skill set to good use.

To this point, I am pleased to report that there has been no dead air.